Sport and Social Media in Business and Society

This concise, practical book examines the significance of social media for the sport industry, explaining key concepts and sharing tools and best practice for the use of social media in sport business communication.

Accessibly written and avoiding jargon, the book considers the history, development, commercial impact, social effects, and the legal and ethical concerns of social media in the context of sport. Covering all levels of sport, from professional to grassroots, the book includes international cases and examples throughout, presenting key findings from current research. It also explains the role of social media agencies and the fundamentals of managing a sport organization's social media platforms and outputs.

This book is essential reading for all sport business professionals and for any sport business, management, or marketing student looking for a primer on this important and growing subject.

Gashaw Abeza is recognized as one of the leading scholars in the field of social media in sport. He is Associate Professor at Towson University, USA, and a member of the editorial board of nine different academic journals. Dr. Abeza serves as a sport management consultant in different countries, and he is a Research Fellow and Doctoral Advisor at Munich Business School, Germany.

Ryan King-White is recognized as one of the leading scholars in the field of physical cultural studies. He is Associate Professor of Sport Management in the Department of Kinesiology at Towson University, USA. Dr. King-White has expertise in a range of socio-cultural topics, including global sport spectacles, intercollegiate athletics, youth sport, qualitative research methodology, and critical pedagogy.

Routledge Focus on Sport, Culture and Society

Routledge Focus on Sport, Culture and Society showcases the latest cutting-edge research in the sociology of sport and exercise. Concise in form (20,000–50,000 words) and published quickly (within three months), the books in this series represents an important channel through which authors can disseminate their research swiftly and make an impact on current debates. We welcome submissions on any topic within the socio-cultural study of sport and exercise, including but not limited to subjects such as gender, race, sexuality, disability, politics, the media, social theory, Olympic Studies, and the ethics and philosophy of sport. The series aims to be theoretically-informed, empirically-grounded and international in reach, and will include a diversity of methodological approaches.

Available in this series:

On Boxing
Critical Interventions in the Bittersweet Science
Joseph D Lewandowski

Sport, Forced Migration and the 'Refugee Crisis'
Enrico Michelini

Sport Policy Across the United Kingdom
A Comparative Analysis
Edited by Mathew Dowling, Spencer Harris and Chris Mackintosh

Olympic Laws
Culture, Values, Tensions
Mark James and Guy Osborn

Sport and Social Media in Business and Society
Gashaw Abeza and Ryan King-White

For more information about this series, please visit: www.routledge.com/Routledge-Focus-on-Sport-Culture-and-Society/book-series/RFSCS

Sport and Social Media in Business and Society

Gashaw Abeza and
Ryan King-White

LONDON AND NEW YORK

First published 2024
by Routledge
4 Park Square, Milton Park, Abingdon, Oxon OX14 4RN

and by Routledge
605 Third Avenue, New York, NY 10158

Routledge is an imprint of the Taylor & Francis Group, an informa business

© 2024 Gashaw Abeza and Ryan King-White

The right of Gashaw Abeza and Ryan King-White to be identified as authors of this work has been asserted in accordance with sections 77 and 78 of the Copyright, Designs and Patents Act 1988.

All rights reserved. No part of this book may be reprinted or reproduced or utilised in any form or by any electronic, mechanical, or other means, now known or hereafter invented, including photocopying and recording, or in any information storage or retrieval system, without permission in writing from the publishers.

Trademark notice: Product or corporate names may be trademarks or registered trademarks, and are used only for identification and explanation without intent to infringe.

British Library Cataloguing-in-Publication Data
A catalogue record for this book is available from the British Library

ISBN: 978-1-032-41501-7 (hbk)
ISBN: 978-1-032-41504-8 (pbk)
ISBN: 978-1-003-35839-8 (ebk)

DOI: 10.4324/9781003358398

Typeset in Times New Roman
by Apex CoVantage, LLC

Contents

About the Authors	*vi*
Preface	*viii*

1	The Basics of Social Media and Sport	1
2	Social Media and Sport Business	20
3	Social Media Platforms Management	37
4	Social Media and Traditional Media	53
5	Social Media and Legal and Ethical Issues	67
6	Social Media and Social Issues	84
	Index	*103*

About the Authors

Gashaw Abeza is recognized as one of the leading scholars in the field of social media in sport. He is Associate Professor at Towson University, USA, and a member of the editorial board of nine different academic journals. Dr. Abeza serves as a sport management consultant in different countries, and he is a Research Fellow and Doctoral Advisor at Munich Business School, Germany.

Before joining TU, he taught graduate and undergraduate students at Southern Methodist University, USA, and the University of Ottawa, Canada. He was a visiting research fellow at the University of New South Wales (Australia), University of Guelph (Canada), and Addis Ababa University (Ethiopia). Dr. Abeza has a long-standing and ongoing research program studying the impact of social media on the sport industry and its implications for society at large. He has written extensively on the topic, publishing more than 70 journal articles and book chapters, and five books.

Currently, Dr. Abeza serves on the editorial boards of nine different academic journals: *Communication & Sport*; *International Journal of Sport Communication* (IJSC); *Journal of Sport, Business, and Management*; *Journal of Relationship Marketing*; *International Journal of eSports Research*; *Journal of Global Sport Management*; *Sport Marketing Quarterly*; *International Journal of Sports Marketing and Sponsorship*; and *Sport Management Digest*. He also serves as an ad hoc reviewer for several academic journals and guest edited two special issues (2018 and 2023) for IJSC on the topic of social media in sport studies. Prior to returning to academia, Dr. Abeza had a successful career in sport business management at a global level and currently provides consultancy services to a range of sport organizations around the world.

Ryan King-White is recognized as one of the leading scholars in Physical Cultural Studies (PCS). He is Associate Professor of Sport Management in the Department of Kinesiology at Towson University, USA. He earned his MA and PhD from the Sport Commerce and Culture program at the University of Maryland – College Park and a BA in Sport Management from Ithaca College studying under such respected scholars as David Andrews, Michael Silk, Jaime Schultz, Stephen Mosher, and Ellen Staurowsky.

Dr. King-White has expertise in a range of socio-cultural topics, including global sport spectacles, intercollegiate athletics, youth sport, qualitative research methodology, and critical pedagogy. Each of these topics has been approached and influenced directly and indirectly by the Birmingham Center for Contemporary Cultural Studies requirement for radically contextual, conjunctural dialecticism. This means using a variety of methodological, epistemological, and axiological approaches to understand present cultural concerns. In lay terms this means critically utilizing as much information and evidence that can be procured from myriad sources to truly understand a particular cultural phenomenon, including, but not limited to, history, qualitative and quantitative observations, and praxical (that is, actually being a part of the study) ways of developing knowledge(s).

He has edited a book and more than 20 peer-reviewed journal articles and book chapters. His articles have been awarded as the article of the year in the *Sociology of Sport Journal* (on the politics of representation of youth sport celebrity), as well as an article designated as a *For the Sociology of Sport* (on the use of critical pedagogy) spotlight article meant to define a key theoretical issue in the field. He is a NASSS Research Fellow in recognition of his contributions to the sociology of sport. To date, fewer than 30 people have achieved such an appointment.

Preface

We are thrilled to share with you our insights into the intersection of sport and social media. In today's world, social media has become an essential part of every industry, including sports. It has transformed the way we consume and interact with sports content, providing unprecedented access to athletes, coaches, teams, leagues, fans, etc.

In our book, we cover the basics of social media, including how it works and how it has revolutionized the way we communicate. We also delve into the business side of social media and how it is reshaping the sports industry, from brand management to sponsorships.

We explore the art of social media platforms management, discussing transformations in social media usage, the evolving practice of managing social media platforms, and practical guidelines in social media management. We also examine the relationship between social media and traditional media, including how social media has disrupted the traditional media landscape.

Furthermore, we address the legal and ethical issues surrounding social media and sports, such as privacy concerns, intellectual property rights, and the impact of social media on athletes' mental health.

Finally, we examine the socio-political concerns related to social media and sports, including the role of social media in activism, social justice, and promoting inclusivity and diversity.

We hope our book provides valuable insights into the ever-evolving world of sport and social media, and helps you navigate the challenges and opportunities presented by this exciting landscape.

Thank you. Enjoy the read.

Gashaw Abeza and Ryan King-White
Summer 2023

1 The Basics of Social Media and Sport

Over the past decade, social media has revolutionized the way sport entities, such as athletes, coaches, fans, teams, leagues, events, media, and sponsors, communicate and engage with their stakeholders. The exponential growth of social media platforms such as Facebook, YouTube, Instagram, TikTok, Twitter (now known as X), and Reddit, has enabled sport entities to reach wider audiences by providing real-time updates, sharing behind-the-scenes content, and connecting on a more personal and authentic level. Similarly, social media platforms have transformed the ways in which users consume content and challenged sport entities to formulate strategies to deal with negative comments, handle misinformation, protect brand image (Abeza et al., 2019), respond quickly to crises (Pegoraro & Frederick, 2021), and manage privacy and security concerns. Clearly, advancements in social media have had a significant impact on the sports industry and have inspired growing interest among scholars and practitioners to examine the impacts of social media on the evolution and future of the sports world.

The significance of social media in sports has evolved in complexity and ubiquity. The purpose of this chapter, therefore, is to discuss some of the fundamentals of social media and lay the groundwork for insights on sport and social media. Specifically, the chapter covers the basics of social media, including its definition, platform types, history, current trends, defining characteristics, and user types. It also covers the numerous issues and concerns that have arisen as sport entities have been able to reach wider audiences, communicate and engage on a more personal level, promote their brand, increase their revenue streams, and change the way consumers absorb content. These issues and concerns revolve around socio-cultural and legal issues, diversity and inclusion, and crisis communication. The chapter concludes with a discussion on the rapidly changing and future trends of social media in the sports industry.

The Expansion of Social Media

The term "social media" encompasses a broad range of platforms, including social networking sites such as Facebook, LinkedIn, and X, multimedia

DOI: 10.4324/9781003358398-1

sharing sites such as Instagram, YouTube, and TikTok, blogs and forums, messaging apps, such as WhatsApp and Messenger, and more. In the simplest terms, social media refers to online platforms that allow users to create, share, and exchange information, opinions, and content with others. Social media is built on the principles of user-generated content, user participation, and social interaction. In this book we define social media as

> online resources open to the public (e.g., blogs, social networks, content communities, and discussion sites) that people use primarily to share content such as text, photos, audio files, and videos, and engage in multi-way conversations on Internet applications (e.g., Facebook, Twitter, YouTube).
> (Hull & Abeza, 2021, p. 4)

In terms of this definition, it is clear that the Internet and mobile devices have played a crucial role in the expansion of social media due to their unique features and capabilities. Some of the ways in which the Internet and mobile devices have facilitated the growth of social media include Internet features such as low cost, convenience, global functional ability, and low set-up and entry costs. Low-cost mobile devices, such as smartphones, iPad/tablets, and portable laptops, have experienced phenomenal growth, and the Internet has become more accessible to large numbers of people. In tandem with the growth of these mobile devices, their operational speed on and off the Internet has increased considerably. Easy accessibility to the Internet and the wide range of devices available has made it possible for individuals and businesses to set up, create, and access social media platforms, and to interact with others from all over the world at low cost or with minimal investment. The Internet has made social media platforms highly convenient to use. Users can access social media from their homes, offices, or on the go, making it easy to stay connected with others and engage with content.

The Internet has allowed social media to become a global phenomenon, connecting people from all over the world. Social media platforms such as Facebook, X, and Instagram have attracted millions of users from different countries, cultures, and backgrounds and enabled instant contact between people who live continents apart. The Internet has also made it easier and more affordable to set up and enter the social media market. Unlike traditional media, social media platforms do not require significant investments in equipment, infrastructure, or distribution. The economy, portability, functionality, and compact design of mobile devices have enabled users to access social media almost anywhere at any time. Through such devices, users can not only interact with friends, family, and business associates, but can also form their own cyber communities.

Three main factors have spurred the global growth of social media in recent years, enabling it to connect individuals from different parts of the world. It has also changed the ways users communicate, interact, and participate in society. These factors are (1) technological drivers, (2) economic drivers, and (3) social drivers. The development of technology has been one of the major forces behind the recent rise in popularity of social media. Improved Internet access, mobile devices, cloud computing, artificial intelligence, and machine learning are among these technological drivers. Today, social media platforms distribute content more quickly and effectively due to the widespread use of high-speed Internet, and the development of handheld devices has made it simpler for users to access social media on the go, leading to higher engagement and usage. Social media companies have been able to increasingly store and maintain enormous volumes of user data as a result of cloud computing, which enables them to offer users personalized and targeted content. Moreover, improvements in machine learning and artificial intelligence have enabled social media platforms to analyze user data and behavior to deliver more relevant content and advertisements.

The economic benefits of social media have been another key driver of its expansion. Advertising revenue, e-commerce, job creation, and investment are a few of the economic stimuli behind its widespread popularity. Businesses use social media to reach out to and interact with customers, and social media platforms generate revenue through advertising. Businesses use social media to advertise and promote products and services, making social media platforms significant e-commerce channels. Social media has also given rise to new professions and vocations in industries such as digital marketing, content development, and social media management. Furthermore, investors have made large investments in social media platforms due to the potential for growth and revenue generation.

The expansion of social media can be also attributed to the social benefits it offers. Social movements, content production and sharing, social connectivity, and digital-community development are a few examples of social drivers. By enabling social connectivity, the platforms empower users to connect with others from all over the world, creating novel possibilities for social interaction and networking. By facilitating users' ability to create and share content, the platforms make it easier for individuals to express themselves and share their experiences with others. Social media has played a significant role in driving social movements and promoting social change, enabling individuals and communities to mobilize and raise awareness of social issues. The social media platforms have also enabled the formation of online communities centered around issues, hobbies, and shared interests, which has facilitated community building. Simply put, a combination of technological, economic, and social factors has contributed to the expansion and development of social media platforms. Abeza and O'Reilly (2018) also found that comparable but distinct drivers have contributed to the rapid expansion of social media.

The Emergence and Growth of Social Media

The emergence of social media can be traced back to the 1990s, when people began to connect and exchange information online through early platforms such as bulletin board systems and online forums. These platforms' ability to expand was constrained by the decade's limited technologies, such as non-portable devices and slow Internet speeds. In fact, the introduction of the World Wide Web in the 1990s prompted the development of the earliest social networking websites, including Six Degrees and LiveJournal, which allowed users to create profiles, connect with friends, and share content such as music and images. The development, expansion, and rise of social media took off in the early 2000s with the launch of sites such as Friendster, LinkedIn, MySpace, Hi5, Flickr, Facebook, and YouTube. These platforms provided users with new ways to connect with others, share information, and build online communities.

Facebook's debut in 2004 marked a pivotal turning point in the rise of social media. Facebook was first only accessible to Harvard students, but it quickly expanded to other colleges and eventually opened to the general public in 2006. Facebook has become the dominant social media platform since the mid-2000s owing to its user-friendly interface and cutting-edge features, such as the newsfeed. Other leading social media networks – X, YouTube, LinkedIn, and Instagram, to name a few – also emerged around the same period (see Table 1.1). As social media expanded in popularity, each platform provided its own distinct features and user base, and social media became an essential component of millions of people's everyday lives by offering a way to remain in touch with friends and family, exchange opinions and observations, and discover new information. The mid-2010s saw the rise of platforms such as Snapchat and Instagram, which became very popular among younger users. In the early 2020s, social media continues to evolve and shape our lives and society. New platforms such as TikTok are rapidly gaining popularity, while established platforms such as Facebook, YouTube, LinkedIn, and X continue to dominate the social media landscape. Many social media platforms have come and gone over the years, and new ones continue to emerge. Table 1.1 presents a list of ten major (first movers and/or popular) social media platforms.

Table 1.1 Major Social Media Platforms

Year Introduced	Social Media Type
1997	Six Degrees
2003	LinkedIn
2004	Facebook
2005	YouTube
2005	Reddit
2006	Twitter (X)
2010	Pinterest
2010	Instagram
2011	Snapchat
2018	TikTok

1997 – Six Degrees: Six Degrees, which debuted in early 1997, is regarded as the first social networking platform.

2003 – LinkedIn: Early in 2003 LinkedIn was introduced, and today is used mainly for job seeking and professional networking. LinkedIn features job listings and company pages.

2004 – Facebook: Launched early in 2004, Facebook was and is currently the most popular social networking platform in the world. It enables users to make profiles, stay connected with people they know, join groups, and exchange different types of data, such as text postings, pictures, and videos. Facebook offers a newsfeed in which users can view updates from pages and people they follow.

2005 – YouTube: Introduced early in 2005, YouTube quickly took over as the most popular site in the world for uploading and sharing videos. Users can watch and share other people's videos and create and upload their own. A variety of content is available on YouTube, including music videos, movie trailers, tutorials, and vlogs.

2005 – Reddit: Introduced in the middle of 2005, Reddit has garnered about 100 million followers, who regularly visit its discussion forums. These forums cover a variety of distinct groups or "subreddits," devoted to a wide range of subjects. To encourage discussion and dialogue, users can publish content, leave comments, and vote on posts and comments.

2006 – Twitter (now known as X): Launched in late 2006, Twitter quickly became popular for its 280-character "tweets," which are short messages. Twitter is a micro-blogging service that enables users to communicate with their followers by sending them brief messages or "tweets." These tweets include text messages, images, and videos, which are frequently used to disseminate news and updates.

2010 – Pinterest: Introduced in early 2010, Pinterest is a visual bookmarking platform that enables users to store and organize photographs and other types of content. Users are mostly interested in collecting and exchanging image collections or "pins" on digital pinboards.

2010 – Instagram: Late in 2010, Instagram was introduced. It is geared largely toward sharing photos and videos, with a focus on visual content. Users create profiles, follow other users, and receive reciprocal followers. Instagram's stories feature photos and videos users share before their stories disappear from the Feed after 24 hours, unless users add them as a highlight.

2011 – Snapchat: Snapchat was introduced in 2011. This messaging site allows users to post photos and videos (known as "snaps") that disappear from the site after a set number of seconds. Additionally, users can put their "snaps" in a sequence viewers can watch as a "story."

2018 – TikTok: Launched in 2018, TikTok is a video-sharing social media platform. TikTok is traditionally set to music, with users lip-syncing or dancing along with the song. Starting with its United States debut in 2018, TikTok has been popular mainly amongst younger audiences.

As social media has grown, it has come under increased criticism for misinformation (Di Domenico et al., 2021), privacy and security (Jain et al., 2021), cyberbullying (Chan et al., 2021), and other issues. To allay these concerns, social media corporations have reported to have launched new policies to enhance data privacy controls and content moderation. Despite these challenges, social media has profoundly altered the way users connect, communicate, and consume content. Social media continues to have a significant impact on how individuals conduct their lives and how modern society is shaped.

Social Media Platforms

Social media platforms have common attributes, such as (1) user profile, (2) user access to digital content, (3) a user list of relational ties, and (4) user ability to view and traverse relational ties (Wakefield & Wakefield, 2016). The term "social media" has generally been used to describe publicly accessible online resources that enable users to create and share content (such as text, images, videos, and audio files), engage in peer-to-peer communication (through comments, likes, shares, and private messages), connect with like-minded individuals based on shared interests, hobbies, or identities, and build communities. Yet, because social media platforms provide users with a variety of features and capabilities, a particular group of platforms has features and functions that set them apart from other groups. In this regard, Hull and Abeza (2021) classified social media platforms into four major groups: blogs, social networks, content communities, and discussion sites. These platforms are briefly described, along with corresponding sports-related examples.

Blogs: These platforms allow individuals or organizations to create and publish their own content in the form of articles, posts, or videos. Typically, blog posts are displayed in reverse chronological order, with the most recent post appearing at the top of the page. Readers can leave comments on blog posts, creating a two-way conversation between the author and the audience. Since the development of social networks, blogs are now traditionally fan driven and created, including pages for the Seattle Mariners (www.ussmariner.com) and the Toronto Maple Leafs (www.mapleleafshotstove.com).

Social Networks: These platforms are designed for users to connect and interact with each other. They typically feature user profiles, messaging systems, and newsfeeds that display updates from the users' network of connections. Users can share a wide range of content, including photos, videos, and links to external websites. Popular social networks include Facebook, X, LinkedIn, and Instagram. In the sporting context, particularly popular sites are NBA Facebook (www.facebook.com/nba), ESPN's X (@espn), and FC Barcelona's Facebook (@fcbarcelona).

Content Communities: These platforms depend mainly on videos, photos, and audio files from users. They allow users to share their content and interact with others with similar interests. These platforms often have features for rating and commenting on content, as well as tools for organizing and categorizing content. Examples of content communities include Pinterest, Instagram, SnapChat, and YouTube. Some sports-related examples include Cristiano Ronaldo's Instagram (@cristiano), WWE's YouTube Channel, UFC's TikTok (@ufc), and Cristiano Ronaldo's Snapchat (@CristianoRonaldo).

Discussion Sites: These platforms focus on facilitating conversations and debates around specific topics or issues. They typically feature forums or message boards on which users can start or join discussions, ask questions, and share their opinions. Discussion sites can range from niche communities focused on a particular interest or hobby to large forums that cover a wide range of topics. Typical examples of discussion sites include Quora and Reddit. Sports-related examples include the Calgary Flames forum (http://fans.flames.nhl.com/community/) and the New York Giants Board (https://thegiantsboard.proboards.com/).

The Defining Characteristics of Social Media and Its Users

The defining features of social media platforms include the use of real-time communication, community building, user-generated content, interactivity, viral diffusion, user privacy and control, and mobile accessibility. As a real-time communication platform, social media gives users a sense of immediacy and urgency by allowing them to connect in real time. Social media enables individuals to establish online groups based on common identities, interests, or hobbies. As a platform that relies on user-generated content, social media allows users to produce and share text, photographs, videos, and audio recordings. The interactive design of various platforms enables users to communicate with one another through comments, likes, shares, and private messages. The immediacy and open interactivity of social media platforms enable content to spread quickly and easily, potentially reaching a wide audience through sharing and reposting. Users can manage their online appearance and safeguard their personal information by using the platforms' privacy settings and controls over the content they share. Finally, mobile devices are mostly accessible at all times, allowing users to access them on the go.

These defining characteristics have made social media a powerful tool for communication, information sharing, and community building. They have impacted users' level of usage and degree of attachment to a given social media site. A user's level of participation on a social media site may range from passive visits to making committed contributions. Abeza and O'Reilly (2018) noted that some users may visit a social media site multiple times a day every day; others log on much less frequently. One may use some platforms often, but never visit a different social media site. Hull and Abeza (2021) (based on

Harridge-March & Quinton, 2009) grouped social media users into six types in terms of their level of familiarity with and usage of a given site. These are Lurkers, Newbies, Onlookers, Minglers, Devotees, and Influencers (see Figure 1.1).

Lurkers: Users who merely observe social media activity and rarely engage with others are known as lurkers. These users frequently read posts and comments but rarely add anything to the discussion. They would rather remain nameless and just take in information without contributing to the conversation.

Newbies: These are the brand-new, inexperienced social media users. They tend to share content and leave comments on social media, even at a minimal level. These users are still learning about social media and figuring out how to engage better with other users.

Onlookers: These users enjoy observing and following popular personalities, brands, and other influencers on social media. They may like or share content but rarely engage in conversations or create their own content. They usually stay updated on trends, news, and popular culture through social media.

Minglers: These users are very sociable; they converse with others, produce their own content, and engage in social interaction. They enjoy making new friends and interacting with others who have interests similar to their own. They tend to use social media to widen their social networks and build relationships.

Devotees: These users are highly dedicated to a particular brand or personality on social media. They are loyal followers who engage in conversations, share content, and actively promote the brand or personality they admire. They tend to be highly engaged and may even defend their favorite brands or personalities against criticism.

Influencers: These people are the top-tier social media users. They usually have a sizable following and the power to influence others. They frequently make use of their influence to market goods, services, or ideas, and they may work with brands to advertise their goods or services because they are recognized as authorities in their field.

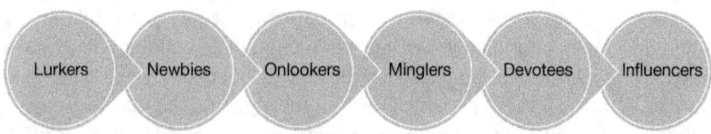

Figure 1.1 Social Media Users Ladder

Source: Adapted from Harridge-March and Quinton (2009)

Social Media and Emerging Issues in Sport

Social Media and Sport Business Management

In today's sports industry, social media has become a critical aspect of fan engagement (Vale & Fernandes, 2018), brand management (Blaszka & Cianfrone, 2021), relationship marketing (Abeza et al., 2020b), sponsorship (Parganas & Anagnostopoulos, 2021), ambush marketing (Abeza et al., 2020a), revenue generation (Achen & O'Reilly, 2021), sales management (Newman et al., 2017), and other similar aspects of sport business management. This section will address the use of social media by some sport entities and present a more thorough discussion in the following chapter. As mentioned in the opening paragraph of this chapter, sport organizations use social media for a variety of reasons. Teams, leagues, athletes, fans, journalists, coaches, events, media, and sponsors are some of these users. Four entities (teams, athletes, fans, and journalists), plus minority sport and the social media profession are discussed in the following sections as examples of how these entities use social media.

Social media serves a multitude of functions for teams and leagues. These include sharing game highlights, streaming games live, delivering behind-the-scenes content, responding to fan questions (feedback and concerns), promoting forthcoming events (merchandise and sponsorships), interacting with fans and followers, and creating a strong community. Social media also enables athletes to engage with their fans, develop personal brands, and advertise their sponsorship and endorsement deals. They share their daily schedules and workout plans, answer fans' queries, and provide glimpses into their personal lives on social media. Social media also allows fans to engage with other fans and share their opinions and views, react to matches, and keep current on the latest news, statistics, and results. Fans also use social media to follow their favorite players, participate in promotions, and stay in touch with teams and leagues. Journalists use social media to keep updated on sports-related information and cover sports news and events. They engage with athletes, coaches, and teams through social media and have access to information that may not be available through conventional methods. Journalists also use social media to promote their work.

Social media also plays an important role in minority (niche) sports, which often struggle to receive attention from mainstream media and acceptance by the general public. Social media offers them a direct line of communication between athletes, teams, and fans. For example, minority athletes using social media can communicate directly with fans from around the world while sharing their experiences and showcasing their talents. Fans can also interact directly with athletes, teams, and fans on social media, which can help build a community around a minority sport. In particular, fans can connect with others who share their love of the sport if they were unable to find a local group of like-minded individuals. As a result, online communities and fan groups may emerge, helping to spread the word about the sport and cultivate a devoted following, which can further build a loyal fan base. Hence, social media professionals promoting minority sports would be expected to have a good understanding of the platforms as well as their respective audiences and functionalities. They should also be familiar with social media analytics and tracking tools to monitor performance and execute effective social media strategies that align with overall objectives.

Professionals should also be knowledgeable about the ethical and legal ramifications of using social media and be conversant with the rules and guidelines of various social media platforms. Therefore, social media experts working for minority sports would be expected to have an in-depth knowledge of the platforms, as well as their respective audiences and functionalities, be familiar with social media analytics and tracking tools to monitor the performance, be able to develop and execute effective social media strategies that align with overall objectives, be able to produce compelling content that resonates with target audiences, and be aware of the ethical considerations. Simply put, in order to effectively use the platforms, a social media professional needs to be well-versed in and have a solid understanding of social media and its function in the sporting industry.

Case 1.1   The Drone Racing League and Social Media

The Drone Racing League (DRL) won the 2022 Sport Business Journal Awards for "Best in Social Media." DRL is a professional racing league for elite drone pilots that was founded in 2015 and headquartered in New York City. This award recognized the DRL's rapid rise in popularity and success in engaging with audiences through its innovative use of technology and social media. Millions of fans watch the races on NBC, YouTube, TikTok, Twitch, X, Instagram, and Facebook. The DRL has been successful in engaging with audiences by leveraging social media platforms such as YouTube, Instagram, X, and Facebook to broadcast its races and engage with fans. Examples of how the DRL uses social media are as follows:

X: The DRL uses X to communicate real-time with fans during races, share race results, and provide news updates. The league also frequently tweets memes and GIFs about drones, which helps keep the content cheerful and enjoyable.

YouTube: The DRL has a sizable following on YouTube with 520,000 followers as of the beginning of 2023. On its channel, the league regularly publishes highlight reels and behind-the-scenes photos. Also, it broadcasts races live on YouTube, enabling viewers from all over the world to tune in and follow the action live.

Instagram: The DRL posts eye-catching pictures and videos of drones in action to its close to 300,000 followers on Instagram. Additionally, it advertises its sponsors, shares sneak peeks of forthcoming races, and highlights the personalities of its pilots on Instagram.

Facebook: The DRL publishes similar content to its Instagram account on its Facebook page, which has more than 1.5 million followers. Additionally, it uses Facebook to advertise forthcoming competitions and interact with fans via comments and direct messaging.

The DRL has been able to expand its audience and boost fan engagement owing to its social media presence. The league has been successful in bringing in a new generation of drone racing enthusiasts by showcasing the thrill and excitement of the sport.

Social Media and Socio-Cultural Issues in Sport

Social media has become a powerful tool for addressing socio-cultural issues in sports, such as gender (Kavanagh et al., 2019), racism (Kilvington & Price, 2019), homophobia (Hansen et al., 2022), religion (AlKhalifa & Farello, 2021), and disability (French & Le Clair, 2018). Social media platforms offer athletes, fans, and other related stakeholders a forum for dialogue, experience sharing, and building awareness of these concerns. This sub-section offers a quick overview of the relevance of social media to socio-cultural issues (e.g., gender, race, homophobia, religion, and disability). Chapter 6 explores this subject in greater detail.

The topic of gender in sport has been the subject of heated debate by stakeholders and participants for a long time. Female participants in sport have experienced various forms of discrimination, including unequal remuneration and limited opportunities. Social media, however, has given female athletes a platform to share their stories, connect with fans, and advocate for greater gender equity in sports. Moreover, it has helped raise awareness of women's sports, which have traditionally received little coverage in mainstream media. Another significant concern – and one that has occupied considerable media attention – is racism in sport, as a result of which athletes of color have been discriminated against both on and off the field. Social media has enabled players to speak out against racism and campaign for greater representation and inclusion in sports. It has also helped uncover incidents of racism in sports and hold individuals and organizations accountable for discriminatory conduct. Sports are also affected by homophobia and discrimination against LGBTQ+ people. Athletes who identify as LGBTQ+ can now advocate for greater acceptance and inclusivity in sports by sharing their experiences and voicing their concerns on social media. Instances of homophobia in sports have also been brought to light, and discriminatory laws and practices have been contested. Religion is another socio-cultural issue in sports, with some athletes encountering discrimination or exclusion based on their religious values or practices. Social media has provided athletes with a platform to raise public awareness about these concerns and campaign for more acceptance and understanding. It has also helped foster diversity and respect for other faith traditions in sports.

Disability is another key topic in sports. Athletes with disabilities have historically experienced impediments to participation and unfair treatment, but they can now interact with others online, share their experiences, and promote increased accessibility and diversity in sports. Social media has also helped promote the visibility of para-sports and challenge stereotypes of athletes with disabilities. In general, social media has been instrumental in bringing attention to socio-cultural issues in sports and in advocating for greater equity, inclusivity, and respect for diversity. By creating a forum for conversation and interaction, social media has empowered athletes, fans, and other stakeholders to bring about positive change in the sporting world.

Diversity and Inclusion in Social Media and Sport

Similar to social media and socio-cultural issues in sport, concerns about diversity and inclusion have become increasingly prominent in sports social media. Multiple ways exist for social media to advance diversity and inclusion in sports through representation, education, community engagement, the use of inclusive language, and policy development. Social media can be a potent instrument for promoting diversity and inclusion by showcasing athletes and teams from various origins. Different social media platforms have been used to highlight the accomplishments of athletes from underrepresented communities. This has inspired young people from various backgrounds to participate in sports and promote awareness of issues relating to diversity and inclusion. Sports fans and followers can now be educated about issues of diversity and inclusion via social media. Sport organizations can make educational materials accessible (in the form of articles, videos, and infographics) on social media that emphasize the value of diversity and inclusion in sports, which helps increase awareness of the importance of an inclusive culture. Social media can be used to interact with various communities and increase inclusivity in sports in terms of community engagement. Teams and organizations can use social media to notify fans and followers about community initiatives that support diversity and inclusion. This fosters a sense of togetherness and common purpose and helps develop connections across various communities.

Social media can also be used to encourage the use of inclusive language in sports, such as using gender-neutral pronouns and avoiding pejorative terminology. Language is a powerful instrument for encouraging diversity and inclusion and could contribute to the creation of a more inviting and inclusive environment and lead to the development of policies that ensure organizations and groups are actively supporting inclusion and diversity. In summary, social media can be a powerful tool for improving diversity and inclusivity in sports. By showcasing diverse athletes, educating fans and followers, interacting with diverse groups, advocating for inclusive language, and developing policies that support diversity and inclusion, sports organizations can create a more welcoming and inclusive environment via social media.

Social Media and Legal Issues in Sport

As noted, social media has impacted the world of sports significantly by becoming a fundamental component of contemporary culture. Yet, sport organizations should be aware that social media can result in legal problems. Defamation, privacy, cyberbullying, contracts, intellectual property, and other similar concerns are some of the legal problems that can arise from using social media in sports. Chapter 5 will examine these and other legal concerns in greater detail; this section will give a brief summary of those issues.

Users can easily and readily express their opinions on social media, which could lead to defamation cases if statements are inaccurate or harmful to another individual or group. Avoiding such scenarios is particularly important for sportspeople and sports organizations that have a public profile. Social media can also serve as a platform for cyberbullying, which has been a major that problem athletes, coaches, and sports organizations across the entire sports spectrum need to address. Social media also poses a real threat to privacy. Anyone with access to shared personal information on social media could commit identity theft or engage in stalking or harassment. Sports teams and athletes should exercise caution when posting information on social media and make sure their privacy settings are safe.

Another domain of which sport entities should be mindful is that concerning contractual commitments. For instance, if a brand sponsors an athlete, the athlete may be legally required to exclusively promote that brand (from its industry category) on social media. A breach of contract could have harmful outcomes for the athlete. In a similar vein, when using social media, sports organizations must be mindful of issues related to intellectual property. Copyright and trademark infringements can occur on social media, and athletes and sports organizations need to be careful to avoid the unauthorized use of trademarked or copyrighted materials, particularly those that include logos, pictures, or videos. In short, social media can benefit sport entities greatly, but it also presents legal issues that require cautious management. Sports entities can continue to take advantage of the power of social media while avoiding legal problems by being aware of the potential hazards and taking the necessary steps to avoid or mitigate them.

Social Media and Crisis Communication in Sport

Social media has become an important tool for crisis communication in the world of sports. In the past, crisis communication was managed primarily through traditional media channels, but social media has now become a critical platform for addressing crises quickly and effectively. Some of the ways social media is used for crisis communication in sport include real-time updates, two-way communication, crisis-response planning, and reputation management. This section will give a brief summary of these elements of crisis communication.

In communicating real-time updates, sports organizations can use social media platforms to share updates on situations as they develop. Updates on the state of injured players, information on postponed or canceled games, and any other concerns impacting the team or organization can all be included in this category. Social media sites are being used to swiftly share information with others and resolve any inquiries or issues stakeholders may have. Social media promotes direct, two-way connection between sports organizations and their fans, which can be especially useful in emergency situations because it allows individuals to seek clarification from the organization/s concerned regarding any rumors or misinformation that may be circulating. Social media can also be used to develop plans for dealing with potential trouble or catastrophes by enabling promoters or brand holders to demonstrate their commitment to transparency and accountability. Social media has evolved into a vital tool for crisis management in the sports industry. Sports organizations may manage crises and maintain the trust of their followers by using social media to deliver real-time updates, engage in two-way direct communication with fans, build crisis-management strategies, manage their reputation, and communicate brand messaging.

Challenges of Social Media in Sport

Social media has brought about a number of opportunities to the sport industry; however, it has also presented an array of challenges that impact various aspects of the industry. These include legal implications, socio-cultural dynamics, and diversity and inclusion endeavors, which are discussed briefly next.

Defamation and Misinformation: Over time, social media platforms have evolved into fertile grounds for the proliferation of defamatory statements and the rapid dissemination of false information. Athletes, teams, and sports organizations face the pressing need to protect their reputations and counter the propagation of inaccurate narratives on these platforms, which, in turn, exposes them to potential legal entanglements.

Data Privacy and Security: Sports entities gather and leverage customer data from social media platforms, a practice that can spark concerns about the integrity of data privacy and security. Breaches of this sensitive information not only carry the risk of legal ramifications but also pose a significant threat to the credibility of the sports organization within the eyes of the public. The potential fallout from a data breach underscores the paramount importance of implementing robust safeguards to protect both the individuals whose data is collected and the organization itself.

Lack of Privacy: Because of social media's widespread use, athletes are subject to greater levels of public scrutiny and intrusion into their private lives. They lose their sense of privacy as a result of this ongoing exposure, which also invites unwanted media attention and unwarranted intrusion. The blurring of boundaries between their professional and private spheres can lead to emotional strain, potentially affecting their overall well-being and their ability to focus on their athletic performance. In the digital age, athletes will be forced to strike a delicate balance between their demand for privacy and their public identity.

Pressure and Mental Health Issues: The ubiquity of social media sheds a persistent focus on athletes, intensifying the weight of expectations to succeed, maintain a carefully designed image, and manage the flood of critique. This excessive pressure puts a toll on their mental well-being, manifesting as heightened stress levels, persistent anxiety, and even grappling with more profound mental health concerns. The social media platforms' demand for instant responses and constant engagement can also worsen these challenges, underscoring the need for proactive measures to support athletes' mental health.

Online Abuse, Harassment, and Cyberbullying: Although social media platforms allow for direct communication between fans and athletes, they frequently turn into hotspots for such behavior. Athletes from disadvantaged origins are disproportionately affected by discriminatory practices including racism and sexism. This has negative psychological effects that foster a toxic online environment. The possibility of cyberbullying and improper fan behavior exacerbates these problems, endangering players' mental health and decreasing fan participation.

Representation, Bias, and Stereotyping: Social media has the ability to both highlight representational gaps in the world of sports and provide a forum for underrepresented perspectives. However, the danger of insincere gestures looms, as they frequently lack the drive to implement significant diversity and inclusion initiatives. Meanwhile, the development of a diverse and equitable sports environment is hampered by the unintentional propagation of stereotypes and biases on social media through negative narratives and biased comments.

Like any other area, social media has both beneficial and negative effects on the sport industry. It is crucial for athletes, teams, and sports organizations to navigate these platforms carefully, assessing the potential advantages against the difficulties they provide. The sport industry may take advantage of social media's opportunities while cultivating an atmosphere that is more inclusive, egalitarian, and responsible for athletes, corporations, and fans by understanding and resolving these shortcomings.

Future of Social Media in the Sports Industry

Social media has developed into a potent instrument in sports, enabling various sport entities to communicate with their fans and maintain long-term relationships. As social media platforms continue to evolve, several trends are likely to shape the future of social media in the sports industry. Some of these (see Table 1.2) include mobile optimization, live streaming, video content, data analytics, artificial intelligence, social commerce, and social media influencers.

Mobile Optimization: This is crucial for social media, as most social media users access the platforms using mobile devices (Pew Research, 2021). Sports organizations must therefore ensure their content is mobile-friendly and that their platforms provide a seamless user experience. Examples include optimizing images and videos for mobile viewing and creating mobile-responsive interfaces.

Live Streaming: The sports industry is experiencing an increase in the use of live streaming (Nielsen, 2023), a trend that is expected to continue. The popularity of live streaming can be attributed to several factors, including the expansion of high-speed Internet access, the widespread use of mobile devices, and sports fans' desire to watch content in real time.

Video Content: The sports industry has experienced a surge in the popularity of video content (Sprout Social, 2023), another trend that is set to continue. Sports entities will likely make greater investments in producing video content to engage viewers and showcase behind-the-scenes footage.

Table 1.2 Trends to Shape the Future of Social Media in Sport

Future Trends	Attributes
Artificial Intelligence	Allowed the examination of data about audiences, their activity, and preferences in order to produce more personalized content
Data Analytics	Enabled the gathering of data to help better understand audiences and develop more targeted marketing campaigns
Live Streaming	Attributed to high-speed Internet access, the widespread use of mobile devices, and desire to watch content in real-time
Mobile Optimization	Need for optimizing images and videos for mobile viewing and creating mobile-responsive interfaces
Social Commerce	Facilitated a more convenient purchasing process such as tickets, merchandise, and other products directly from social media
Social Media Influencers	Need to capitalize on their sizable following, their expertise in a given field, and the power to influence others
Video Content	Attributed to its power to capture attention and trigger emotions more than other content types such as text and photographs

Data Analytics: The sports industry is paying increasing attention to data analytics (Abeza et al., 2022), and social media platforms will have a big impact in this domain. Entities will use social media to gather data about their fans' habits and preferences, which will help them better understand their audiences and develop more targeted marketing campaigns.

Artificial Intelligence: As artificial intelligence evolves, sport entities are likely to employ it to enhance the way they manage social media platforms (PwC, 2023). The management of social media in sport can be improved by using artificial intelligence to evaluate data about fans, their activities, and their preferences to produce more personalized content.

Social Commerce: Social commerce is the practice of selling products directly on social media platforms (Zhou et al., 2013). This practice is becoming increasingly popular (Wang et al., 2022), and sports organizations are increasingly likely to sell tickets, merchandise, and other products directly from social media platforms, which makes the purchasing process more convenient.

Social Media Influencers: The role of social media influencers in sport is growing (Hull & Abeza, 2021), and this trend is expected to continue in the sports industry. Influencers will use their platforms to share their experiences and thoughts with their followers, and sports organizations will work with influencers to promote their events, products, and services.

Given that social media gives sport entities a means of communicating with their followers, it will continue to play a critical role in the world of sport. Hence, sport groups will have to adapt along with social media platforms and capitalize on emerging technologies and trends to gain maximum traction in their market presence. In a similar vein, social media scholarship is going to grow ever more essential in revealing new insight as social media continues to permeate people's lives and fuse well with sports industry.

References

Abeza, G., Braunstein-Minkove, J. R., Séguin, B., O'Reilly, N., Kim, A., & Abdourazakou, Y. (2020a). Ambush marketing via social media: The case of the three most recent Olympic games. *International Journal of Sport Communication, 14*(2), 255–279.

Abeza, G., & O'Reilly, N. (2018). Social, Digital, and Mobile Media in Sport Marketing. In *Advanced Theory and Practice in Sport Marketing* (3rd Edition). New York, NY: Routledge.

Abeza, G., O'Reilly, N., & Braunstein-Minkove, J. R. (2020b). Relationship marketing: Revisiting the scholarship in sport management and sport communication. *International Journal of Sport Communication, 13*(4), 595–620.

Abeza, G., O'Reilly, N., Finch, D., Séguin, B., & Nadeau, J. (2020). The role of social media in the co-creation of value in relationship marketing: A multi-domain study. *Journal of Strategic Marketing, 28*(6), 472–493.

Abeza, G., O'Reilly, N., Nadeau, J., & Abdourazakou, Y. (2022). Big data in professional sport: The perspective of practitioners in the NFL, MLB, NBA, and NHL. *Journal of Strategic Marketing*, 1–21.

Abeza, G., O'Reilly, N., & Seguin, B. (2019). Social media in relationship marketing: The perspective of professional sport managers in the MLB, NBA, NFL, and NHL. *Communication & Sport*, 7(1), 80–109.

Achen, R., & O'Reilly, N. (2021). Revenue Generation and Return on Investment. In *Social Media in Sport: Theory and Practice* (pp. 403). Barcelona, Spain: World Scientific.

AlKhalifa, H. K., & Farello, A. (2021). The soft power of Arab women's football: Changing perceptions and building legitimacy through social media. *International Journal of Sport Policy and Politics*, 13(2), 241–257.

Blaszka, M., & Cianfrone, B. (2021). Social Media and Brand Management in Sport. In *Social Media in Sport: Theory and Practice* (pp. 223–252). Barcelona, Spain: World Scientific.

Chan, T. K., Cheung, C. M., & Lee, Z. W. (2021). Cyberbullying on social networking sites: A literature review and future research directions. *Information & Management*, 58(2), 103411.

Di Domenico, G., Sit, J., Ishizaka, A., & Nunan, D. (2021). Fake news, social media and marketing: A systematic review. *Journal of Business Research*, 124, 329–341.

French, L., & Le Clair, J. M. (2018). Game changer? Social media, representations of disability and the Paralympic games. *The Palgrave Handbook of Paralympic Studies*, 99–121.

Hansen, M., Kavanagh, E., Anderson, E., Parry, K., & Cleland, J. (2022). An analysis of responses on Twitter to the English Premier League's support for the anti-homophobia rainbow laces campaign. *Sport in Society*, 1–15.

Harridge-March, S., & Quinton, S. (2009). Virtual snakes and ladders: Social networks and the relationship marketing loyalty ladder. *The Marketing Review*, 9(2), 171–181.

Hull, K., & Abeza, G. (2021). Introduction to Social Media in Sport. In *Social Media in Sport: Theory and Practice* (pp. 1–28). Barcelona, Spain: World Scientific.

Jain, A. K., Sahoo, S. R., & Kaubiyal, J. (2021). Online social networks security and privacy: Comprehensive review and analysis. *Complex & Intelligent Systems*, 7(5), 2157–2177.

Kavanagh, E., Litchfield, C., & Osborne, J. (2019). Sporting women and social media: Sexualization, misogyny, and gender-based violence in online spaces. *International Journal of Sport Communication*, 12(4), 552–572.

Kilvington, D., & Price, J. (2019). Tackling social media abuse? Critically assessing english football's response to online racism. *Communication & Sport*, 7(1), 64–79.

Newman, T., Peck, J., & Wilhide, B. (2017). *Social Media in Sport Marketing*. New York, NY: Routledge.

Nielsen (2023). *High-Demand Sports and Streaming Content Fuel a Rise in Total TV Usage in January*. https://bit.ly/42DdgiE

Parganas, P., & Anagnostopoulos, C. (2021). Social Media and Sponsorship in Sport. In *Social Media in Sport: Theory and Practice* (pp. 253–286). Barcelona, Spain: World Scientific.

Pegoraro, A., & Frederick, E. (2021). Social Media and Crisis Communication in Sport. In *Social Media in Sport: Theory and Practice* (pp. 345–381). London, UK: World Scientific Publishing.

Pew Research (2021). *Mobile Fact Sheet.* www.pewresearch.org/internet/fact-sheet/mobile/

PwC (2023). *Sports Industry Outlook 2023.* https://pwc.to/2H3gPsG

Sprout Social (2023). *Social Media Video Statistics Marketers Need to Know for 2023.* https://sproutsocial.com/insights/social-media-video-statistics/

Vale, L., & Fernandes, T. (2018). Social media and sports: Driving fan engagement with football clubs on Facebook. *Journal of Strategic Marketing, 26*(1), 37–55.

Wakefield, R., & Wakefield, K. (2016). Social media network behavior: A study of user passion and affect. *The Journal of Strategic Information Systems, 25*(2), 140–156.

Wang, X., Wang, H., & Zhang, C. (2022). A literature review of social commerce research from a systems thinking perspective. *Systems, 10*(3), 56.

Zhou, L., Zhang, P., & Zimmermann, H. D. (2013). Social commerce research: An integrated view. *Electronic Commerce Research and Applications, 12*(2), 61–68.

2 Social Media and Sport Business

Think about the following inquiries for a moment: What effects is social media having on the sports industry? How do sports marketers utilize social media? What effects are social media having on social commerce? What role does social media play in managing the brand of sports? What about its function in endorsement? What effects has social media had on sports sponsorship endorsement? How much of an impact does social media have on ambush practice? How about as a relationship marketing tool? How is social media impacting the practice of customer service? These issues are covered in this chapter, which offer insight into the use of social media in the sport business.

Using social media enables individuals to communicate with a large audience at convenient times, locations, and frequencies. Similar to this, businesses in all sectors are increasingly running social media channels and producing content to engage with their constituents. In this regard, sport is an industry that uses social media as a medium to carry out different marketing endeavors, such as sales, customer service, sponsorship, endorsement, branding, ambush marketing, and relationship marketing. This chapter discusses the use of social media as a tool to implement these different marketing communication efforts. The chapter has three main parts. The first part presents an overview of social media in sport business. The second and the main parts explores social media in sport and social commerce, sport brand management, endorsement, sponsorship management, customer service, ambushing marketing, and relationship marketing. All these will be discussed in the context of athletes, teams, leagues, events, fans, etc. The final part summarizes the points covered in the preceding sections.

Elements of Social Media Use in Sport Business

The sport industry has adopted social media to accomplish a range of objectives. Local community sport organizations as well as youth, professional, collegiate, international, and Olympic sports all use it. It is also used by athletes, coaches, fans, sponsors, and the media. Almost every facet of the sport industry and every entity is impacted by social media. In sport business, sport entities use the different social media platforms (e.g., Facebook, X, YouTube) to communicate content (e.g., text, photo, audio recordings, videos) with their audiences by engaging in a multi-way dialogue. In the communication process, entities use social media as a medium to implement marketing objectives such as sponsorship, sales, customer service, relationship marketing, endorsement, branding, ambush marketing, etc. This chapter discusses how social media can be used in sport business by taking into account the dynamic relationship between sport and social media and recognizing the variety of uses for which it can be put to use.

Social Commerce and Social Media

The increasing popularity of social media is providing new opportunities for businesses in electronic commerce. Many experts think that social media features should be coupled with electronic commerce to enhance trust between buyer-seller transactions and enable the creation of more economic value. Hence, social commerce involves online communities that facilitate user interactions and user-generated content, in contrast to traditional e-commerce, where customers often engage with online shopping sites independently. It is a practice that makes use of web 2.0 technologies and social media to support social-related exchange activities (Han & Trimi, 2018). Social commerce can also be considered as a subset of e-commerce that improves using social media to assist customers in their commerce transactions and activities (Salvatori & Marcantoni, 2015). In practice, social commerce's rise has significantly altered both the corporate and consumer landscapes. Social media is primarily used in social commerce to ease transactions, generate product recommendations, share shopping experiences and evaluations, and leverage social influence to boost sales. Social commerce can have a significant effect on businesses. It can open up a new sales channel, aid businesses in raising brand awareness, and foster customer engagement and loyalty. Additionally, social commerce can help firms expand their reach, enhance the consumer experience, and collect valuable customer data.

Social commerce is highly prevalent in the sports business, especially when it comes to the sale of sporting goods and gear. Fans can now buy jerseys, hats, and other branded products straight from their favorite teams and athletes thanks to the proliferation of sports teams and athletes who have set up their own social media profiles and online shops. Many sports teams and venues allow fans to buy tickets directly through social media platforms, demonstrating the social commerce trend in the sports business. This has facilitated fan ticket purchases and assisted teams and venues in boosting ticket sales. Influencer marketing is another component of social commerce in the sports sector. Sports firms frequently collaborate with athletes and sports influencers to market their goods on social media, taking advantage of their sizable fan bases to boost product exposure and boost sales.

In a series of studies conducted by Abeza et al. (2017), reported that social media is used for selling where it is an attempt to persuade users to purchase merchandise from the teams' stores and tickets to games, or buy signed jersey, balls, and other memorabilia at auctions. Examples include:

@Padres: After Christmas sale at the team store! Store hours are Monday-Saturday 10am to 5pm and Sunday from 11am to 4pm. (Dec. 26th, 2015)
@Jaguars: Rock your Bold at The 'Bank for TNF! Expedited shipping now available for #BeBold gear: http://jagrs.com/BoldRushShop111515 (Nov. 15th, 2015)

Abeza et al. (2017) reported that social media has been used in sport to provide the latest information about a team's ticket sales, ticket discounts, giveaways, contest sweepstakes, giveaways, lotteries and raffles, merchandise sales, players' autograph opportunities, upcoming events, etc. (e.g., @NHLBlackhawks: It's our final day of #HawksHolidays giveaways! Win a trip to the #StadiumSeries in Minny: csnchicago.com/hawksholidays). It is also worth noting here that social shopping, group buying, social recommendations, and social storefronts are a few examples of the assortment of shapes that social commerce can take. Group buying refers to using a large group's purchasing power to obtain discounts or other benefits, whereas social shopping refers to the use of social media platforms to advertise and sell things. Social storefronts relate to the incorporation of e-commerce features into social media platforms, whereas social recommendation refers to the practice of using social networks to recommend goods or services to others.

Customer Service and Social Media

One of the values of social media is its use as a customer service platform, where it serves as a direct line of communication to listen to questions, comments, or concerns, and address them. In the recent past, when there is any concern, the first place consumers come to get a direct and immediate response to their requests is social media. It also helps gauge overall customer satisfaction. Particularly, unlike traditional customer service mediums such as toll-free numbers, social media helps address the requests of a particular fan, and on the way that response simultaneously reaches out to many others with similar interests. Hence, the fans feel that they have an impact on not only their experience but also someone else's when we answer back to them. The real-time and direct customer service could be assistance with in-stadium services (e.g., parking, traffic, and concessions) and technology (e.g., broken web links, online access, mobile applications), replies to questions about games, inquiries about a player's injury, and contest clarifications. This value of social media as a customer service platform is essential, in particular, as fans today want their issues to be resolved quickly with easy-to-find solutions. Most significantly, it enables teams to have satisfied fans, which improves fans' enjoyment of sports and, thus, improves fan identification. The following examples from Abeza et al. (2017) of social media from the Red Sox and Broncos illustrate the case:

@craignicoll16: @RedSox could you tell me If/when there would be tickets for the games v yankees in September might become available to purchase
@RedSox replied: @craignicoll16 Yankees tickets will become available after a drawing for the opportunity to purchase. Likely within the next 2 months.
@Broncos: .@DEN_Broncofanss wanted a #Peyton-signed football. Wish granted, thanks to @Arrow Global! What's your #BroncosWish?
@alison_maclean replied: @Broncos @ArrowGlobal my #BroncosWish is a sideline pass for Sunday. Traveled from Scotland to the US for the first time for #SDvsDEN
@Broncos replied: @alison_maclean DM us when you can! Your #BroncosWish is in the works!

Simply put, it is a widely recognized fact that social media is a medium that is beneficial to fans expressing their views and enabling teams to comprehend their followers' continuously shifting needs owing to social media's speed, ease of access, and public forum aspects. Fans therefore value the possibility social media offers to communicate directly with teams about any customer experience–related issues, as well as the ability to access real-time customer service via social media and share the team response with a larger audience who may be experiencing a similar problem.

Brand and Social Media

A brand can be defined as a name, logo, or other outward symbol that distinguishes a product or service from others in its category. Since a brand can be communicated physically and emotionally, consumers know a brand first by its brand name, which can be one or more words (Los Angeles Lakers), a logo or trademark (the Nike swoosh), or a sound representative of the brand name (the Liverpool Football Club associated song, "You'll Never Walk Alone"). These are elements of a brand, and a brand is the most valuable intangible asset of an entity at a corporate, product, or individual level. Think of strong sport brands such as LeBron James, Dallas Cowboys, La Liga, All Blacks, FIFA, the Olympics, ESPN, Adidas; fans of these sport properties engage with these brands on a variety of levels throughout their daily lives (e.g., proudly wearing the jersey of a favorite player, wearing a team's scarf, singing a team song, having a team's logo as their Facebook profile picture, etc.). In the past decade, social media has become essential in sport brand management.

The parallel relationship between sport entities' brand value and the size of social media followers is only one illustration of how quickly social media is evolving and has become increasingly interconnected with sport branding nowadays. The most valued sport entities today are, for instance, leaders on social media platforms, highlighting the value of social media in brand management. For example (keeping in mind that the number of followers may change over time, as of April 2023): Nike, one of the world-leading sportswear manufacturers, is a leader on Instagram among competitors with 280 million followers; Cristiano Ronaldo, one of the most famous sports personality in the world, is the most-followed person on Instagram with 566 million followers; Real Madrid, one of the world-leading sport team brands, is the most-followed sport team on social media with 117 million followers on Facebook. Hence, sport brands must continue to be adaptable, responsive, and authentic in their content and messaging given the increasing prominence of social media. At the same time, social media has created new challenges that call for careful planning and execution, such as handling negative comments or damage to one's online reputation.

In fact, the ultimate goal of brand management is increased brand equity. A brand equity is assets and liabilities linked to a brand name that add to or subtract from that product's value (Aaker, 1991). A brand, therefore, enjoys a high level of brand equity when the following components of brand management are prominent: brand awareness, brand associations, perceived brand quality, and brand loyalty. To briefly describe these components – following O'Reilly et al.'s (2022) work – in relation to social media, let's take the Los Angeles Lakers as an example:

- Brand awareness: Brand awareness could be, for example, the Lakers' social media profile, its logo, colors (purple, gold, black), its motto, or content communicated on the organization's X, Facebook, and Instagram sites to help users learn more about the team's performance, high-profile players, merchandises, services/goods, and the organization.
- Brand associations: Brand association could be the unique attributes of the brand that are communicated on social media to consumers. In other words, what comes to one's mind when they think of the Lakers, which can be Kobe Bryant, the city of Los Angeles, the Staples Center, NBA championships, the playoffs, Laker Nation, Celtics rivalry, etc.
- Perceived brand quality: Perceived brand quality could be the large following and popularity of the Lakers, which is the most-followed NBA team on X with 11.4 million followers. Also, the Lakers are always perceived as a team with a strong potential for the playoffs. In connection, the perceived quality of a brand can be increased by engaging with fans on social media, acknowledging their support, and responding to their inquiries.

- Brand loyalty: Brand loyalty could be displayed on social media in different ways, such as changing a profile picture to one with a Lakers logo or a picture of a favorite player. On the team side, social media can be used to enhance and maintain team loyalty by creating a Facebook group for avid fans, including season ticketholders. The team can produce graphic design works and short video clips that facilitate the display of loyalty on social media.

Brand equity is the sum total of the efforts put into the previous four components of brand equity. Sport entities have created, re-created, developed, maintained, extended, and advanced their brands for years and will continue to do so in the future. As a result, it is critical to manage a brand so that it conveys the idea that the target market(s) wants to associate with. In this regard, social media has become essential in sport brand management in the past decade. Also, social media can be used to release a new brand (e.g., the release of the 2022 documentary *Legacy: The True Story of the LA Lakers*) or to rebrand a property (e.g., Crypto.com Arena from Staples Center). Moreover, social media has given athletes new opportunities to nurture and better manage their personal brands. Athletes can communicate with their fans on social media, give details about their personal lives, and advertise their sponsorships. In order to attract sponsors, boost their marketability, and build a devoted fan base, athletes might utilize social media to display their personality, hobbies, and ideals, which help build their personal brands.

Case 2.1 Building Manchester United's Brand Through Social Media

Manchester United Football Club is a perfect example of how to use social media to boost brand equity in the dynamic world of football branding. The Manchester United brand is a combination of both assets and liabilities. A narrative that resonates across digital platforms is created through the interaction of brand elements such as awareness, associations, perceived quality, and loyalty.

Brand Awareness: On social media, Manchester United's colors – red and white – shine bright in their logo. Look at Instagram, X, and Facebook, and you will find these colors. It is like a flag that waves, saying, "This is Manchester United!"

Brand Associations: Social media shares stories about Manchester United's past, making people think of great players such as Wayne Rooney and exciting times in Old Trafford, their famous stadium. Think of Manchester city – the place – and how it is alive with football history.

Perceived Brand Quality: Lots of people follow Manchester United on social media. This is like a badge of honor. It means lots of people like them. On Instagram, the club is one of the top five most-followed teams in the world with 62.6 million followers as of summer 2023. This tells us they are seen as the most valuable sport brand in the world.

Brand Loyalty: Manchester United fans across the world show their love to the team on social media by using the team logo or player pictures as their profile pictures, and Manchester United loves back by sharing special things with fans.

A new level of fan involvement is created by the reciprocal engagement between Manchester United's brand and social media. Its status as a worldwide phenomenon – a brand that thrives on shared history, present moments, and future aspirations – is solidified as a result of this intertwining, which raises the club above the level of a simple football team.

Sponsorship and Social Media

Sponsorship is defined as an investment, in cash or in kind, in an activity, with an expectation for a return on investment, which sets in a three-way relationship between the sponsors, the sponsored party, and consumers. Sport receives the largest portion of all sponsorship dollars in North America (70%), mostly because it is an ideal medium for engaging sponsors in an emotional connection with consumers. In other words, customers will be drawn to a sponsor that backs a sport product or service they like and support. Particularly, when presented through a sport property that is sponsored by a company, consumers feel that corporate messages are less intrusive and have a goodwill effect. Social media is the ideal tool for sponsor efforts since it can best support the emotional bond that fans develop with a sporting property. As was already noted, social media is a participatory and collaborative platform, giving sponsors the opportunity to interact with fans directly and humanize their brands.

Social media serves as an effective method for sponsors to connect with customers owing to its widespread use, reach, and distinctive features. Speed, accessibility, real-time functionality, connectivity, and a public forum are some of the distinctive aspects. Sponsors will have the chance to communicate regularly with customers through social media, control the communication's tone, use brand personalities, and humanize their companies. Social media also has the built-in ability to act as a social hub for users who have similar needs and desires as well as similar interests in a particular sport. Moreover, social media has the power to draw in large numbers of followers with similar interests to the platforms, and thus, aggregate reachable target audiences of a particular sport.

It is an industry-wide agreed-upon practice that sponsorship is much more than simple logo placements, and sponsors need to invest in activation to realize the full potential of their sponsorship investment. When a sponsor engages in a contract with a sponsored party, the sum of money they pay for a particular asset is simply for them to have a legal right of affiliation. For example, when Crypto.com took the naming rights or entered into venue sponsorship of the formerly known Staples Center, the money that the cryptocurrency platform and exchange pays to the arena is only to have the right to an official association and to publicly announce that the platform is sponsoring the venue. But, in order to promote and inform their sponsorship to the wider public, Crypto.com needs to invest more money on advertising such as billboards, TV commercials, digital engagement, hospitality arrangements, experiential opportunities, etc. And, most importantly, using social media. This type of initiative is referred to as sponsorship activation. Simply put, activation is additional investment beyond the rights fee or different communication efforts implemented to support one's sponsorship.

Activating a sponsorship on a property's social media platforms enables a sponsor to reach people who are receptive to marketing communication initiatives surrounding the sport. Using hashtags, creating promotional campaign messaging, and interacting with event followers are social media tactics that can increase the success of the activation. Some suggested strategies include creating engagement opportunities such as a photo competition among participants about their best experiences with a sponsor's product or service or having a 30-second video testimonial from a specific subset of attendees about a sponsor. Using their own social media platforms, sport properties can also provide sponsors an added venue to publicize their association through appreciation of their support, promoting their services/products, and sponsors' gestures.

A social media post can be also "boosted" (by paid communication) to reach new audiences on the platform in addition to those who follow the property's social media channels. As a part of these activations, innovative social media content, like carefully thought-out graphic design and embedded video clips, can be created to promote a sponsor. As noted, in addition to connecting naturally with followers, this information can also be promoted with various calls to action, such as "like us," "follow us," "comment now," "learn more," and "share now," with the goal of creating awareness that results in impressions, shares, and likes (O'Reilly et al., 2022). To increase likes and shares, as O'Reilly et al. (2022) pointed out, content can be attached to these calls-to-action, such as testimonials, visit-website links, chat-now offers, and contact-us information. Relatedly, to encourage purchase, content can be attached (with links) to calls-to-action such as "add to cart," "add to wish list," "download coupon," and "see related products."

Furthermore, a property can assist a sponsor in achieving its goals through the utilization of its social media platforms. Particularly, sponsors can interact directly with fans (of the sport property) on social media because it is a participatory and collaborative platform, allowing them to attach their brands to the property and perhaps even engage fans. In this context, one strategy for sponsors is to "humanize" their brand by having a conversation with the sport property that is personable, warm, and humorous. Building and maintaining relationships with the audiences of the sport property can be made possible by communicating directly with customers.

Ambush Marketing and Social Media

Consider the following situation for a moment: Let's say you run a café in a small college town that sponsors a high school basketball team. In the town, there is another café with which yours is in fierce competition. Every other Saturday, the high school basketball team you sponsor plays at home. As the team's official sponsor, you place banners from your café around the high school basketball court and entrance, post updates to your Facebook and Instagram pages, and hand out brochures and vouchers to attendees of the event. Also, you air a weekend local radio ad wishing your sponsored team good luck. During those home games, the rival café, which is not officially affiliated with the basketball team, also posts a discount and coupons to those who attend the games on its Facebook and Instagram pages, airs a radio ad wishing the same team good luck, and sends out a handful of young spectators with advertising boards, who display the boards whenever the home team scores. Would you approve of the competitor café's actions at the event and on the radio, if you were the sponsoring café? Why? The action of the non-sponsoring café is referred to as ambush marketing. Simply put, the practice of non-sponsoring companies' attempt to associate themselves with an event without having an official or direct commercial connection is referred to as ambush marketing (Abeza et al., 2020b). This section covers the practice of ambush marketing via social media.

Non-sponsoring firms usually devise creative strategies to benefit from the visibility, goodwill, and other advantages that come with major events such as the Olympics. Companies that have not paid for a range of major events that they are wanting to connect themselves with may be found. Some people view that practice as unethical, whereas others see it as a clever marketing strategy. Regardless of the point of contention, businesses participate in ambushing techniques primarily to gain from the popularity and widespread media attention of a sponsored property. The cost of sponsorship fees, exclusivity, and the length of the sponsorship arrangement are additional variables that encourage businesses to engage in ambushing. Nonetheless, ambush marketing may cause official sponsors to become irate and frustrated, and the practice may endanger the sponsorship sector (e.g., sponsorship renewals). Sport governing bodies established various protection mechanisms to address the problem. The three most common counter-ambush strategies include (Abeza et al., 2020b): (1) legislation – law to punish parties found involved in ambushing practice,

(2) communication – increasing public awareness about event properties, including trademarks, and (3) surveillance – identifying intellectual property infringement. Even with these tactics, planning an event without an ambush is still challenging (Abeza et al., 2020). Social media in particular gave ambushers a new platform to apply their inventive marketing tactics. Social media's capabilities, such as its information flow and capacity to bypass border barriers, make it difficult for the activity to be regulated by institutional or national boundaries (Abeza, 2020).

Recently, the main competitors of the sponsors of important sporting events have been engaging in a number of ambushing activities on social media platforms. Following this, international sporting organizations such as the International Olympic Committee (IOC) and FIFA (the world's governing body of soccer) implemented a social media ambush protection regulation. For instance, the IOC used Rule 40 to prohibit athletes from identifying themselves with non-official Olympic sponsors before, during, and immediately after the Games, despite the IOC encouraging players to use social media during the games to share their experiences with relatives and friends. The IOC, specifically, issued social media guidelines that include tweets and various other Internet postings in 2014, 2016, 2018, and 2020 (Abeza, 2020). In light of these guidelines and protection strategies, According to Abeza et al. (2020), non-sponsoring businesses continue to use social media for the practice of ambush marketing. Based on their research, the authors identified the following four categories of ambush marketing techniques used on social media:

- Values Ambushing: Values ambushing is the practice of implying an association by utilizing the central theme of a property. The direct industry competitors of the Olympic sponsors have been observed utilizing Olympic-related themes to attract social media followers. An example is Pirelli, where the company employed value ambushing by communicating a tweet with pictures that revolve around the Winter Olympics' central value of racing on a snowy downhill slope: "When you are late for a meeting, but you have a @Lamborghin#WinterChampion."
- Property Infringement: Property infringement involves the deliberate unlicensed use of trademarked intellectual property, such as a logo, a name, or words. In this strategy, for example, Subway offering "congratulations" to participating teams or athletes with the mention of Olympic names and words, and Ford communicating a congratulatory message using a protected Olympic term.
- Coattail Ambushing: By using a trustworthy connection, such as participating athletes, coattail ambushing is seeking to establish a direct affiliation with a property. It was observed that the direct industry rivals of the Olympic sponsors were making direct associate with the Games by means of a valid connection, such as competing athletes Olympians. An example is Subway's use of X during the Rio Games, when the company retweeted

the NBC Olympics X account with Aly Raisman's USA gymnastics performance. In the retweet, Subway used the caption "NBC fresh focus presented by @subway." It should be noted that NBC had a legitimate partnership with the Olympics as an official broadcaster; however, instead of directly seeking a sponsorship with the Olympics, Subway engaged its brand with NBC to "piggyback" off its legitimate link to the event.

- Associative Ambushing: Associative ambushing is the use of images or phrases to imply that an organization is connected to the event. For example, Michelin employed associative ambushing during the PyeongChang Games by tweeting: "The UK snow has got us in the mood, so we've taken a look at the top 10 snowboarding videos on the internet! – https://sole-power.com/skiing-snowboarding-spring/: : : " with a picture of a skier taking a break from training on a field covered with snow and having his skates by his side. Keep in mind that the time of the tweet is important in this case, given that the item in question was tweeted during the Olympic Games.

Research has shown that ambush marketing via social media occurs regularly around major events (Abeza et al., 2020). Direct competitors within the same industry were observed using four distinct ambush methods: associative, values-based, coattail, and property infringement. The results show how ambush marketing strategies have evolved over time, moving from overt distraction, confusion, and breaching the law to more opportunistic-focused, deceptive, and sophisticated marketing communication practices. The identified four strategies suggest that the unique characteristics of social media (e.g., no border restrictions, no time barrier, viral, easy access, public forum) are expanding the territory for ambushers to carry out their inventive marketing initiatives, even with host countries' laws and the IOC's social media guidelines in place. Specifically, since institutional gatekeepers or national boundaries can rarely halt the flow of information on social media, it has developed into a crucial platform for ambushers in their capacity to participate in breaking time and border limits. The production of an ambush-free event is challenging due to the hazy legal definitions, astute strategies developed by non-sponsors, and the new level of convenience that social media gives for reaching the target market.

Endorsement and Social Media

Today, a number of celebrity athletes, such as LeBron James (e.g., with Hummer "CrabWalk"), Canelo Alvarez (e.g., with Tecate), Cristiano Ronaldo (e.g., with Armani), and Stephen Curry (e.g., with Under Armour) are using their celebrity status (e.g., names and image) to endorse products and services in advertising in an exchange for financial rewards. Meaning, in using their social media platforms for endorsement purposes, celebrity athletes are transferring their celebrity status (e.g., names and image) to the brand they are endorsing. The question is, therefore, what is a celebrity endorser? A celebrity endorser is an individual "who enjoys public recognition and who uses this recognition on behalf of a consumer good by appearing with it in an advertisement" (McCracken, 1989, p. 310). Exceptional sportspeople represent athletic achievement and the ideals of a thriving sport culture. Primarily, the symbiotic and interdependent relationship between the media and professional sport contributes significantly to elevating athletes to a status that is almost mythical in society. Famous athletes are worldwide brand identities, and marketers leverage celebrity athletes' attractiveness to promote both sporting and non-sporting goods, as well as their likeable and trustworthy character to positively affect consumers' buying decisions.

Over the past few decades, utilizing famous athletes to promote products has become more common. Particularly, in contrast to the conventional approach, when broadcast media served as the primary communicator of athletes' brands and marketing initiatives, athletes now create, shape, and convey their own brands and marketing initiatives through their own social media channels. Star athletes may attempt to transfer their "symbolic meaning" to a brand partner by using their social media networks for the purpose of endorsements. This can be done by having direct, ongoing, one-on-one conversations with the athletes' followers in real time, with or without the assistance of a third party (such as the broadcast media). Due to the "personal" nature of celebrity athletes' social media endorsements, potential customers' perceptions of the brand partner can be more strongly affected by the athletes' reputation, likeability, believability, attractiveness, and trustworthy persona as well as the emotional attachment that the athletes' fans typically develop with them. Such effects may have a greater impact on fans who appreciate and identify with a specific athlete. Due to these possibilities, social media has become an effective platform for communicating endorsements.

A follow-up question will, therefore, be: how are celebrity athletes using their social media platforms for the purpose of product endorsement? In this regard, Abeza et al. (2017) studied the world's highest-paid athletes' use of their own social media channel for the purpose of endorsement and identified the different roles and modes that celebrity athletes displayed in their endorsement of brands on social media. The five various roles that the highest-paid athletes took on while endorsing brands on social media include acting as an expert, an ambassador, a personifier, a spokesperson, and an observer. The brief description of each role along with the corresponding examples are provided as follows:

- As an expert, an athlete's account can be discovered advocating a product about which they have authoritative information (e.g., LeBron James tweeting about his Nike Air Zoom Generation 1 and asking people to try it).
- As an ambassador, an athlete is advertised as an authorized spokesperson for a brand about which they may not have extensive understanding but

which they have a strong material relationship with (e.g., Chris Paul, an American professional basketball player, posting an Instagram post about State Farm, the insurance company with which he partners).
- As a personifier, an athlete endorses a product that is presented as an embodiment of the athlete's own personal motto and/or professional qualities, which are typically embedded in the brand's campaign message (e.g., American professional basketball player Kevin Durant's "Dream Fearlessly" with American Family Insurance: "@AmFam I want to inspire kids to lead healthier lives #DreamFearlessly").
- As a spokesperson, an athlete acts as an informal representative/advocate of a cause or product with which the athlete has no official association (e.g., Bubba Wallace, an American motorsports racing driver, tweeting about racial inequality and voicing his concern).
- As an observer, an athlete makes a simple, positive public comment about a product but does not communicate any recommendation to try or use it (e.g., Stephen Curry, an American professional basketball player, posting on X a picture of him purchasing food at a food store with the mention of the store's name).

Four endorsement modes are highlighted in relation to the modes assumed by celebrity athletes while endorsing products on social media. These modes are explicit ("I endorse this product"), implicit ("I use this product"), imperative ("You should use this product"), and co-presentational (simply appearing with the product). The following list offers examples of each of these modes:

- Explicit mode: In an explicit mode, a social media post communicates an athlete's endorsement of a product on X (e.g., Rafael Nadal about Drasanvi: "Happy to start working with @Drasanvi and take part in their #health & #wellness projects. Take a look http://t.co/GtzV8QqzgW #NadalDrasanvi").
- Implicit mode: In an implicit mode, a social media post informs social media followers that the athletes are consumers of the endorsed product (e.g., Maria Sharapova, a Russian retired professional tennis player, about Avon: "My secret to natural beauty is out thanks to @AvonInsider! Learn more: a link to Avon's website").
- Imperative mode: In an imperative mode, a social media post encourages fans to try and use the endorsed product (e.g., Usain Bolt about Puma: "The right energy is everything. Get it on February 10th. #ForeverFaster @PUMA http://t.co/CujtPgACT7").
- Co-presentational mode: In a co-presentational mode, the athlete is presented with the product in pictures or videos, or the brand/organization's name is simply mentioned in the tweet (e.g., Bianca Vanessa Andreescu, a Canadian professional tennis player, tweeting a picture of her taken standing next to a car she drives).

Case 2.2 LeBron James: Social Media's Role in Brand Building

LeBron James stands as a globally renowned athlete, recognized for his exceptional success. His stature has attracted endorsements from prominent brands such as Nike, McDonald's, Microsoft, and Kia Motors. He features prominently in commercials and campaigns for these brands. As of Summer 2023, his Instagram (@kingjames) boasts 157 million followers, while his X (@KingJames) and Facebook (@LeBron) have 52.7 million and 27 million followers, respectively, totaling a staggering 236.7 million followers.

LeBron is not solely an athletic icon but also an influencer of unparalleled impact. Beyond his sports achievements, he has harnessed his social media presence to craft a powerful brand. He employs his platforms to promote endorsed brands, offering his vast number of followers' insights into his off-court endeavors. With an ever-growing follower count, LeBron has found an ideal public relations platform that expands his reach with each new follower. In essence, LeBron's social media presence is not just an extension of is persona; it is an integral facet that boosts his brand to new heights.

Relationship Marketing and Social Media

While social media is a valuable resource to carry out the different marketing communications elements, it predominantly is an effective vehicle for achieving relationship marketing goals (Abeza et al., 2020). Relationship marketing is an approach that is built on establishing, maintaining, and enhancing mutually successful relationships, where value is created for all parties (Achen & Abeza, 2021). It is a process of communication and interaction that leads to value creation, which eventually retains consumers through the long-term mutual satisfaction between businesses and consumers. The building of collaborative relationships through communication and interaction between organizations and their stakeholders involves fulfilling promises, building trust and commitment where two parties, on an ongoing basis, talk to each other, listen to each other, learn from each other, become familiar with each other, and in due course, reach a common understanding (Grönroos, 2004). When organizations reach an understanding with their stakeholders by fulfilling promises they made in their communications and interactions, they would be able to produce and deliver a co-created, customer-valued product (Abeza et al., 2020). In maintaining and enhancing this process on a continuing basis, organizations understand stakeholders' ongoing needs, build intimacy, develop long-term relationships, and ultimately secure long-term mutual benefits (Grönroos, 2000). In this regard, social media provided novel directions to a relationship marketing approach.

An extensive study conducted on the role of social media as a relationship marketing tool in sport by Abeza et al. (2020) bases itself on three sources of multi-dimensional evidence (social media platform, organization, consumers). These sources include (1) conducting a netnographic study of the X accounts of 20 professional sport teams in the four major leagues in North America, (2) conducting semi-structured interviews with 26 senior marketing managers of sport teams in the four major professional sport leagues in North America, and (3) employing sequential, funnel-based focus groups of 10 with 81 participants. This study reported that there are several commonly shared uses of social media across the three domains (i.e., fans, platforms, organizations). The shared uses of social media include news updates, content delivery, customer service, promotional offers, enriching brand identity, humanization, and interaction. From these eight uses of social media, the three sources of evidence informed us that social media is primarily used for interaction purposes (by both consumers and organizations), followed by news updates and customer service. In interacting on social media in real-time, organizations and consumers are talking and listening to each other, and engaging in an ongoing dialogue. Through continuing dialogue, a variety of consumer needs can be met and potentially translated into the building, maintenance, and enhancement of relationships. Further, organizations will have the opportunity to learn about the changing needs of their consumers from these interactions.

For the purpose of updates, social media is used as a source of quick and fresh information, which is accessed before, during, and following a service experience. As a content delivery tool, social media allowed organizations to bring consumers closer through the provision of exclusive stories and enabled consumers to gain access to unique behind-the-scenes content that was difficult to access in the past. Customer service is one of the main benefits that social media offers to both business and consumers. It serves as a direct line of communication to listen to questions, comments, or concerns, and address them. As a means of providing access to personnel, social media offered the opportunity to interact in real-time and directly with an organization through the Q&As with key personnel, which was not common in the past. In terms of enriching brand identity, social media, as a hub for consumers, serves as a venue where conversations about an organization are carried out among highly engaged consumers. As a means of humanizing a brand, social media helps sport organizations to humanize their brand through showing personality (e.g., jokes and funny pictures), engaging in a friendly tone, and creating a closer relationship through personalization (e.g., personalized birthday wishes to consumers).

The creation of value in relationship marketing emerging through communication and interaction is adding greater/extra value to the core service offering, where social media allows organizations to communicate and interact with consumers, understanding the ever-changing consumer needs, carrying on a continuing dialogue, delivering on promises, and in due course, delivering co-created value. Consequently, this enables the development, maintenance, and enhancement of long-term relationships between organizations and consumers. Accordingly, social media platforms are facilitating the co-creation of value, and most of these co-created values, or "extras" to the core service offering, that consumers perceive to be important, beneficial, and unique are specific to social media. As such, social media helps mitigate the challenges that many businesses currently face, such as maintaining a loyal and enthusiastic customer base and fostering greater consumer engagement and discontent with the competition.

Summary

As you have read, social media and the business of sports have a dynamic interplay, as is illustrated in the discussion thus far. This relationship will become more entangled and intense in the course of the coming years, underscoring the essential role that social media plays in sport marketing. Thus far, the use of social media in sport business has certainly revolutionized how the industry is conducted. Its influence can be seen in areas such as sales, branding, sponsorship, endorsement, ambush marketing, relationship marketing, and customer service. It has had a significant impact on sport management. In light of this, social media has developed into a vital instrument for sport managers. Some of the insights on these developments in social media for the sports industry are provided in this chapter.

References

Aaker, D. (1991). *Managing Brand Equity*, New York, NY: The Free Press.
Abeza, G. (2020). The Evolving #Rule40 of the Olympic Charter: Balancing the Interest of Sponsors vs Athletes. In Chatziefstathiou, D., Garcia, B., & Seguin, B., (Eds.). *International Handbook of Olympic and Paralympic Games*. New York, NY: Routledge.
Abeza, G., Braunstein-Minkove, J., Séguin, B., O'Reilly, N., Kim, A., & Abdourazakou, Y. (2020). Ambush marketing via social media: The case of the three most recent Olympic Games. *International Journal of Sport Communication, 14*(2), 255–279.
Abeza, G., O'Reilly, N., & Braunstein-Minkove, J. R. (2020b). Relationship marketing: Revisiting the scholarship in sport management and sport communication. *International Journal of Sport Communication, 13*(4), 595–620.
Abeza, G., O'Reilly, N., Finch, D., Séguin, B., & Nadeau, J. (2020). The role of social media in the co-creation of value in relationship marketing: A multi-domain study. *Journal of Strategic Marketing, 28*(6), 472–493.

Abeza, G., O'Reilly, N., Seguin, B., & Nzindukiyimana, O. (2017). Social media as a relationship marketing tool in professional sport: A netnographical exploration. *International Journal of Sport Communication, 10*(3), 325–358.

Achen, R., & Abeza, G. (2021). Relationship Marketing in Sport. In Pedersen, P. (Ed.). *Encyclopedia of Sport Management*. London, UK: Edward Elgar Publishing.

Grönroos, C. (2000). Creating a relationship dialogue: communication, interaction and value. *The marketing review, 1*(1), 5–14.

Grönroos, C. (2004). The relationship marketing process: Communication, interaction, dialogue, value. *Journal of Business and Industrial Marketing, 19*(2), 99–113.

Han, H., & Trimi, S. (2018). A fuzzy TOPSIS method for performance evaluation of reverse logistics in social commerce platforms. *Expert Systems with Applications, 103*, 133–145.

McCracken, G. (1989). Who is the celebrity endorser? Cultural foundations of the endorsement process. *Journal of Consumer Research, 16*(3),310–321.

O'Reilly, N., Seguin, B., Abeza, G., & Naraine, M. (2022). *Sport Marketing: A Canadian Perspective* (3rd Edition). Windsor, ON, Canada: Human Kinetics.

Salvatori, L., & Marcantoni, F. (2015, July). Social commerce: A literature review. In *2015 Science and Information Conference (SAI)* (pp. 257–262). IEEE.

3 Social Media Platforms Management

This chapter covers the strategic management of social media platforms in sport industry. Over the past two decades, social platforms have been upgrading their features and presence (e.g., Facebook Live in 2016), and streamlining their business operations and revenue generation (e.g., Facebook's Sponsored Stories in 2011). With these advancements and our society's familiarity with the platforms, the practice of managing social media platforms has also evolved. While it started with the method of trial-and-error, the management has advanced at all levels, ranging from ordinary citizens' use of social media to connect to friends to multinational companies, including sport, setting up a social media internal department. Specifically, the chapter covers transformations in social media usage, the evolving practice of managing social media platforms, and practical guidelines in social media management in sport industry.

Transformations in Social Media Usage

Over time, social media usage has undergone tremendous transformation. It has changed from primarily being a tool for individuals to serving as a strategic business medium for large organizations. To name a few trends (as can be seen in Figure 3.1), social media was initially embraced by regular people, after which corporate pages appeared and corporations began to manage social media informally. Following that, organizations began to recognize the value of social media for businesses, and social media management has gradually become professional. In line with this, social media platforms grew in popularity while they were progressively included into overall marketing strategies, which in turn benefited from the adoption of advanced tools and technologies. Due to these trends, businesses today place a strong emphasis on data-driven decision making and the integration of social media with organizational objectives.

Early adoption by individuals: The early adoption of social media platforms by individuals was primarily driven by the desire for personal

DOI: 10.4324/9781003358398-3

38 Social Media Platforms Management

Figure 3.1 Transformations in Social Media Usage

communication, networking, and sharing content online. Platforms such as Facebook, X, and LinkedIn were intended to help people connect with one another and exchange updates and thoughts. One of the main factors contributing to social media's rapid expansion was how easily one could create and share content. People may experience and share moments from their daily lives in real-time using photographs, videos, and texts with (as discussed in Chapter 1) the aid of portable devices such as smartphones and high-speed Internet. Social media has grown into a popular platform for expressing oneself and exchanging experiences with others. As social media platforms gained popularity, they became an essential part of modern human communication and eventually developed into potent tools for connecting with clients and promoting brands for businesses and organizations. For example, in North American major league sports, the Sacramento Kings was the first team from the four major professional sports leagues to join X (January 2007), and it took the Arizona Cardinals four years as the last team from the four major professional sports to join X (October 2011).

Emergence of business pages: The emergence of social media business pages began in the mid-2000s with the popularity of sites such as Facebook and LinkedIn. As social media platforms evolved and gained more features and capabilities, businesses began to create dedicated business pages on these platforms. In the early stages of a business's social media presence, companies created company pages and shared updates, deals, and news with their followers. As social media platforms grew in popularity, businesses were able to develop direct contact lines with their customers by setting up a social media presence. This allowed them to exchange information, get feedback, and instantly respond to client issues. Additionally, social media gives companies the chance to showcase their goods or services to a larger audience, enhancing their brand recognition and boosting sales. Later, businesses began utilizing features such as paid advertising, influencer marketing, and social listening as social media platforms developed in order to more efficiently reach their target audience.

Informal social media management: In the early days of social media, businesses often approached social media management informally and without a clear strategy. Individual employees or small teams would often handle this ad-hoc strategy; while these personnel might have had some prior social media experience, they frequently lacked the expertise or resources needed to create a thorough social media strategy. They posted content sporadically and without a clear strategy or plan in place. Over time, businesses tried out various strategies and tactics in an effort to figure out what would work best for their brand and target market. Some businesses relied on conventional marketing strategies and used social media only as an extra channel for message distribution. Others engaged with consumers directly through social media, offering support, replying to inquiries, and responding to feedback in real-time.

Recognition of social media's business value: As social media platforms continued to grow in popularity, businesses started to realize their considerable business value. Companies have realized the potential of social media as a potent instrument to foster customer service, brand management, drive sales, advertising, public relations, sponsorship, etc. Simply put, social media has evolved into an essential component of contemporary business, and companies that understand its importance are better positioned to thrive in the current digital environment.

Professionalization of social media management: With the increasing recognition of the business value of social media, businesses gradually became aware of the necessity for a more formal approach to social media management and the need for establishing specialized social media teams or departments. Setting up a specialist department for social media management and developing thorough social media plans that complemented the organization's larger business objectives became a vital part of a company's marketing communication strategy. Such departments are often in charge of handling the company's social media presence, developing and implementing social media strategies, producing content, interacting with clients, and measuring the outcomes of social media initiatives.

Integration of social media into overall marketing strategy: Social media management evolved from being an isolated function to being integrated into the overall marketing strategy of companies. To provide a consistent and unified approach across all marketing channels, social media departments regularly collaborate with other marketing functions such content marketing, digital marketing, and branding. Hence, social media platforms management has gradually become interconnected with other departments of a company such marketing, sales, and customer service, and by being allied with other marketing channels (such as email and search engine optimization).

Case 3.1 All Blacks' Integration of Social Media Into Overall Marketing Strategy (2015)

In 2015, the New Zealand All Blacks rugby team showcased the seamless integration of social media into their overarching marketing strategy, not only enhancing their on-field triumphs but also cultivating a strong and lasting connection with their fan base worldwide.

Engaging the Sixteenth Man

Recognizing the growing influence of social media, the All Blacks harnessed the power of content creation to forge an even deeper connection with their fans in 2015. Legendary figures such as Jonah Lomu and Richie McCaw featured prominently in campaigns for Heineken and Dr. Dre, respectively, amassing millions of views and likes. Air New Zealand's innovative safety campaign further underscored their prowess in the digital arena.

A Social Brand Beyond Boundaries

All Blacks transcended national borders, boasting a Facebook following that rivaled even the Rugby World Cup's at the time (in 2015). Their digital dominance, with 4.5 million followers across various platforms, firmly positioned them ahead of rival rugby-playing nations.

Fan-Centric Content Marketing

Central to their social media campaign was the "We Belong" initiative. Seamlessly blending Kiwi culture with innovative digital design, the All Blacks engaged diverse audiences around the themes of sport and cultural unity. Fans were invited to join the ranks of #TeamAllBlacks, opening access to exclusive content and behind-the-scenes insights. The campaign effectively fostered connections through inclusive messaging and an array of social media touchpoints.

Taking the Team Nationwide

Under the "Taking the All Blacks to the Nation" program, the team embarked on an extraordinary journey that extended beyond the norm, visiting towns and communities that rarely experienced such a spectacle. This initiative deepened the players' connection with their fans and emphasized their resolute commitment to the nation. By interacting with everyday New Zealanders, the team solidified their status as national heroes.

Global Brand Building Through Narrative

Adopting a compelling narrative approach, the All Blacks embraced their role as global rugby legends. Similar to Brazil's enduring significance in football, they positioned themselves as the pinnacle of rugby excellence. This narrative was deftly carried into uncharted markets, cultivating a magnetic allure and an aura of mystique. Despite their reputation as formidable opponents, the brand's undeniable charisma drew adoration and loyalty from fans worldwide.

In essence, the All Blacks' content marketing strategy, carefully integrated with social media tactics, embodied the evolution of integrating social media into comprehensive marketing strategies. Through captivating content and effective fan engagement exercises, they emerged as a model of successful integration.

Source: Eberl (2015)

Adoption of advanced tools and technologies: With the growing complexity and scale of social media management, companies began implementing modern technologies and tools to streamline their social media management and improve efficiency. Social media management platforms, analytics tools, content creation tools, and scheduling tools are among the technologies adopted by social media departments to optimize their efforts.

For instance, social media management tools make it easy for companies to manage all of their social media accounts in one place, streamlining the process of creating, scheduling, and distributing content across several channels. These tools also offer data analytics and reporting options that aid companies to measure the impact of their social media initiatives. Also, tools for creating content have grown in popularity as businesses try to produce high-quality, compelling material that appeals to their target audience. With the help of content creation tools, businesses can easily and quickly produce videos, pictures, and other sorts of content that can be posted on various social media platforms. Another essential piece of technology used by businesses to automate their social media management procedures is scheduling software.

Focus on data-driven social media management: As social media management has become more complex, companies have recognized the need to make data-driven decisions to optimize their social media efforts. Social media departments can assess the effectiveness of their strategies and adjust for better performance by measuring and analyzing various social media metrics. The engagement rate, reach, impressions, conversions, and other data may all be measured and analyzed by social media departments. For instance, engagement rate gauges the percentage of followers who engage with a brand's content by liking, commenting on, or sharing a post. Reach counts how many individuals view a company's content, whereas impressions count how many times a piece of content is displayed. Conversions reflect the number of people who perform a desired action, like clicking on a website or making a purchase. Social media departments can use these tools to track metrics across various social media platforms to gauge performance over time. Additionally, the tolls offer insightful data on audience behavior and preferences, allowing businesses to target their social media efforts and improve engagement more effectively.

Integration of social media with business objectives: Social media departments are no longer isolated entities within companies. Instead, they transformed into strategic allies of the company's objectives, working in the pursuit of specific business goals and driving business outcomes. As a result, social media is no longer just a tool for communicating with customers or a way to develop relationships with them; rather, it is now an essential component of a company's business strategy, with the aim of achieving objectives including raising brand awareness, generating website traffic, creating leads, and growing sales.

In summary, social media usage has undergone tremendous transformation over time. It has evolved from being used by ordinary people for personal communication to large corporations creating internal social media departments to achieve business goals. Hence, its management has transformed from being informal and ad hoc to being more formalized, strategic, and data-driven.

The Contemporary Practice of Social Media Management

The practice of managing social media platforms has gone through various changes and advancements to keep up with the ever-evolving digital landscape. The contemporary practice of social media management (as shown in Figure 3.2) involves content creation and curation, segmenting audience and personalization, data-driven social media management, paid advertising, influencer marketing, social listening and monitoring, online community management, a strategic approach, and platform-specific expertise. Each of these practices will be briefly discussed next.

Content creation and curation: Social media platforms have become increasingly content-driven, and managing these platforms requires creating and curating high-quality content that attracts and retains the target audience. The creation of original content that is tailored to a particular platform and audience is a part of content creation. This includes, but is not limited to, producing images, videos, infographics, live streams, stories, polls, quizzes, and other forms of content. In addition to being informative, visually appealing, and shareable, the content ought to include a clear call to action to encourage engagement. With the introduction of tools such as live streaming, stories, and augmented reality filters, content creation has also broadened in scope.

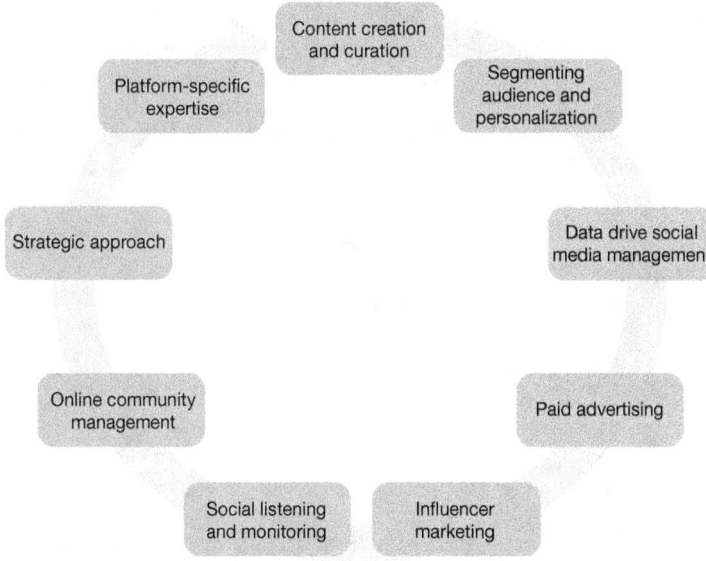

Figure 3.2 The Contemporary Practice of Social Media Management

By extension, this entails the need for understanding the nuances of different platforms, optimizing content for each platform, and staying updated with the latest trends and algorithms. In addition to creating original content to share with their audience, social media managers curate content from numerous sources. This can include relevant content from users, influencer partnerships, and industry news. The goal is to give the audience useful and varied material while establishing the brand as an authoritative source in its specialized domain.

Segmenting audience and personalization: Audience segmentation and personalization have become more important aspects of social media management over time. Today's social media managers may properly segment and target their audience based on demographics, interests, behaviors, and other factors owing to improved targeting features. Instead of using a one-size-fits-all strategy, the features enable social media managers to tailor their messaging, advertisements, and content to the preferences and needs of their target audience. This allows for more effective messaging and personalized communication with the audience, leading to higher engagement and conversions. By segmenting the target audience, social media managers will be able to understand the specific characteristics and needs of various audience groups. The managers may then adjust their messaging and content to be more appealing and relevant to a specific target audience, which will lead to greater engagement and conversions. To understand user preferences and deliver personalized content, social media managers may use data from user interactions, such as likes, comments, and shares. Another aspect of audience targeting and personalization is the use of dynamic content, where social media managers can send followers tailored offers, recommendations, or messaging depending on their location, browsing history, or previous interactions with a business. This allows for a more tailored and relevant experience for each user, increasing their engagement and interest in the brand.

Case 3.2   Chicago Blackhawks: Engaging X Strategy for Fan Connection

The Chicago Blackhawks made proficient use of their X account for the purpose of fan engagement, taking cues from their overall account management approach. They engaged with fans actively, adding a personal touch by incorporating humor, wit, and relevant comments when communicating with fans and sharing updates. Their interactions covered a wide array of topics, from casual chats to answering questions, rewarding fans, expressing gratitude for support, discussing their team slogan, and responding to content requests.

> This interaction approach played a significant role in fostering various positive attributes of fan engagement. The Blackhawks demonstrated genuine enthusiasm for their players, team achievements, and their fan community. Their messaging had a friendly, entertaining, and enthusiastic tone. Notably, they often used humor to present key players, encouraging fans to join in on shared jokes. Players were integral to the fan experience cultivated by the account, acting as catalysts for discussions.
>
> During games, their X comments go beyond basic play-by-play and statistics. They included quick, entertaining, and insightful remarks that added value to the on-ice action. The team also utilized X's diverse features, such as embedding short videos, images, GIFs, and links. The extent of interactions on the Blackhawks' X account was consistent both on game days and non-game days.
>
> Source: Abeza et al. (2017)

Data-driven social media management: Social media management has become increasingly data-driven, due to the availability of data, sophisticated analytics tools, and the need to make educated decisions for effective social media marketing campaigns. To gauge the success of their campaigns and make data-driven decisions, social media managers track and analyze a wide range of performance metrics, including engagement, reach, impressions, and conversions. Some of the aspects of data-driven social media management include audience segmentation, sentiment analysis, trend forecasting, data-driven content development, and performance evaluation. As mentioned earlier, audience segmentation aids in ensuring that social media activities are pertinent to the audience by helping to adapt content and messaging to particular segments. Similar to this, social media managers track and assess conversations and sentiments surrounding a post using data-driven tools and technologies, which can inform future content creation. In a similar vein, social media managers may predict future trends, user behaviors, and outcomes using predictive analytics based on historical data, which helps managers stay one step ahead of the competition. In keeping with this, the other component of data-driven social media management is the creation of content that is informed by data. One can identify the type of content that resonates with the target audience using data pertaining to user preferences and engagement metrics, for instance. This might entail optimizing the timing, frequency, and format of the content for maximum engagement. The effectiveness of social media campaigns can also be evaluated by social media managers using key performance indicators (KPIs) such as reach, engagement, click-through rates, and conversion rates, which helps make data-driven decisions on which campaign is working effectively and which one needs adjustments.

Paid advertising: Paid advertising has become an essential component of social media management due to social media's sophisticated targeting options (such as the ability to precisely target ideal customers and tailor messages), better reach and engagement (such as when displayed in users' newsfeeds and delivered with call-to-action buttons), measurable results (such as the availability of metrics on impressions, clicks, conversions, etc.), and flexibility and scalability (such as a relatively easier budget and ad format adjustment). Therefore, it is now expected of social media managers to be knowledgeable about paid advertising mediums such as Facebook Ads, Instagram Ads, X Ads, and LinkedIn Ads. This involves coming up with marketing plans, making ads, determining budgets, enhancing targeting, and determining return on investment (ROI). Paid advertising enables companies to efficiently connect and interact with their target market, increase website traffic, and lead generation, and thereby achieve their marketing goals. Paid advertising is anticipated to continue to be an essential part of companies' social media management strategy as social media continues to develop. To remain competitive in the constantly evolving social media landscape, organizations must carefully plan and implement paid advertising campaigns as a part of their overall social media management strategy.

Influencer marketing: Influencer marketing is a type of social media marketing that entails teaming up with people who have a significant following and influence on social media, or "influencers," to promote goods, services, or companies. Influencers often have a dedicated following of keen and devoted followers because they are experts or enthusiasts in a certain niche, such as fashion, beauty, fitness, travel, or lifestyle. Utilizing their influence and reach, social media managers now work with influencers to promote goods, services, or brands. Influencer marketing entails the influencer producing content that promotes the brand or product in an honest and authentic way, often incorporating it into their daily lives or sharing their own experiences with it. Due to the trust and loyalty that influencers have built with their followers, this type of marketing is very effective at raising brand awareness, establishing credibility, and triggering potential sales. Influencer marketing now requires expertise in influencer selection, relationship management, and performance tracking, making it a specialist talent within social media management. To make sure influencer marketing initiatives are in line with the brand's objectives and deliver desired outcomes, they must be carefully planned, carried out, and measured. This entails locating pertinent influencers, negotiating partnerships, managing contracts, and gauging the effectiveness of influencer endeavors.

Social listening and monitoring: Social listening and monitoring techniques are now part of social media management. Modern social media managers utilize sophisticated technologies to monitor social media conversations and keep track of mentions, hashtags, and keywords that are relevant to their company. This enables them to quickly respond to client inquiries, comments, and reviews and gives them invaluable insights into the views, preferences, and feedback of their customers. Monitoring social media sites for mentions, tags, comments, and messages referencing a brand or particular keywords is known as social listening. Businesses can use it to find out what's being said about their brand, competitors, and industry, as well as trends and sentiment. Businesses can get important insights to guide their marketing strategies and make data-driven decisions by listening to what customers have to say. On the other side, social media monitoring entails actively responding to comments, messages, and mentions. This enables companies to interact with their customers, build relationships with them, and deliver superior customer service. The prompt resolution of any unfavorable comments or complaints shows that the company values and cares about its customers. Businesses can efficiently track and analyze social media conversations with the aid of social listening and monitoring solutions. These tools give organizations the ability to collect data and insights to guide their social media initiatives with capabilities such as sentiment analysis, keyword tracking, and social media analytics.

Online community management: Social media platforms have become hubs for online communities, and managing these communities has become a critical aspect of social media management. On behalf of a brand, community management is the process of overseeing and nurturing an online community. It involves monitoring and moderating user-generated content, answering questions, dealing with consumer concerns and complaints, and encouraging constructive community interaction. To prevent spam, harassment, and other inappropriate activity, social media managers establish and enforce rules, monitor content, and establish clear community guidelines. Moderator tools are frequently used by community managers to review, approve, or delete user-generated content, such as comments, posts, and messages. Community managers additionally initiate dialogues, pose questions, and promote discussions inside the community to stimulate positive involvement and forge connections with other community members. In general, community managers serve as the brand's voice, speaking for its principles and character. In their interactions with community members, they establish a consistent tone and voice that is in line with the brand's messaging and keeps all communications positive and respectful.

Strategic approach: As pointed out in the last few stages of the transformations in social media usage (prior section), the approach to managing social media has now become more goal-oriented, planned, and aligned with overall business strategies. A more strategic approach to social media management includes the designing of a comprehensive social media strategy, the development of high-quality content, setting up key performance indicators, and employing data and analytics. The designing of social media strategy includes setting specific objectives and goals, identifying the target audience, performing market research, and developing a content strategy that aligns with a company's business objectives. The development of compelling, high-quality content that is tailored to the target audience is another strategic approach to social media management. This involves conducting audience research to understand their preferences, interests, and behaviors on social media, and creating content that resonates with them. Similarly, setting up KPIs to evaluate the success of social media campaigns and employing data and analytics to track progress and make data-driven decisions is becoming key. Businesses now use social media analytics tools to track performance, measure return on investment, and gain insights into the effectiveness of their social media initiatives. To continually improve their social media presence and accomplish their business goals, companies may use a data-driven approach to optimize their social media strategy, identify trends, and make informed decisions. As such, companies are now spending more time, money, and strategic planning on managing their social media accounts.

Platform-specific expertise: Social media platforms are now more varied than ever, with each platform catering to a different set of demographics, interests, and content formats. For efficient social media management, social media managers must possess platform-specific competencies. Every social media platform has distinct features, audience behaviors, content formats, algorithms, and best practices. It's essential to understand and make use of these platform-specific peculiarities in order to develop an optimized content strategy, target the right audience, handle crises, and measure performance. The ever-evolving social media landscape can be challenging to navigate, but social media managers with platform-specific knowledge can successfully manage social media marketing efforts for companies. In order to stay relevant, it is crucial for social media managers to constantly refresh their understanding and their skills to stay up to date with the latest trends and best practices on each social media platform they manage.

Practical Guidelines in Social Media Management in Sport Industry

Managing social media can be a complex and time-consuming task, requiring a deep understanding of social media platforms, content creation, community management, analytics, and more. The following section offers some helpful advice for managing social media effectively (as seen in Figure 3.3, adapted from the work of Braunstein-Minkove et al., 2021). Persistent effort, monitoring, and adaptation are essential for effective social media management. One may build a strong social media presence for a company and produce significant results by adhering to the following 10 basic practical guidelines.

Define goals: Your social media objectives should be clearly stated and linked with your overall business objectives. Your social media endeavors should be focused on achieving specific goals, whether they be improving sales, generating leads, raising brand awareness, or increasing website traffic.

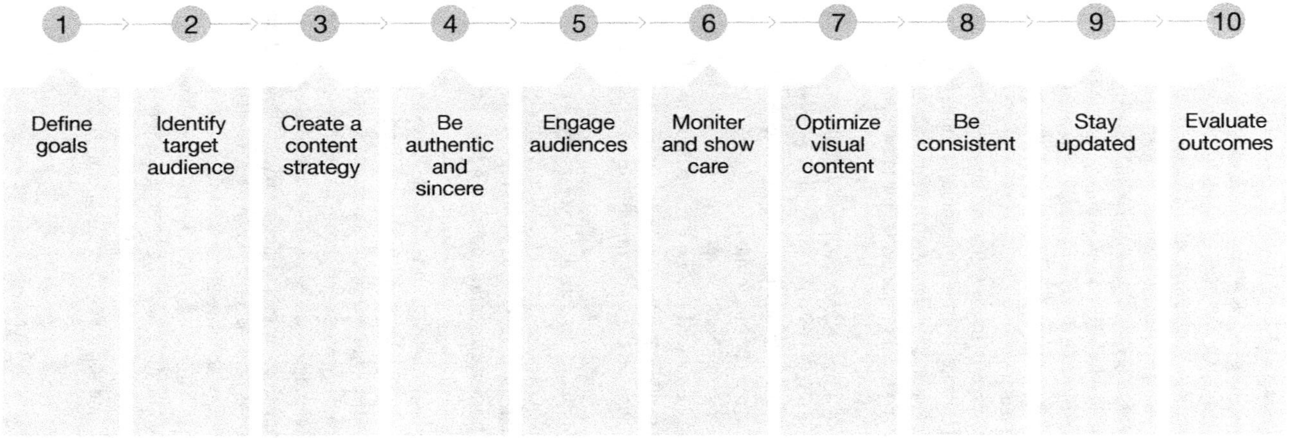

Social Media Platforms Management 49

1. Define goals → 2. Identify target audience → 3. Create a content strategy → 4. Be authentic and sincere → 5. Engage audiences → 6. Moniter and show care → 7. Optimize visual content → 8. Be consistent → 9. Stay updated → 10. Evaluate outcomes

Figure 3.3 Basic Practical Guidelines in Social Media Management
Source: Adapted from Braunstein-Minkove et al. (2021)

Identify target audience: Recognize who your target market is, then adjust your social media messaging and content accordingly. Conduct market research, gather data on the characteristics, preferences, and behaviors of your target audience, and use that data to produce content that appeals to them.

Create a content strategy: Build a content plan that outlines the types of content you will produce, how often you will post, and the platforms you will employ. Your content must be engaging, timely, and in line with the tone and values of your brand. To achieve consistency, plan the contents ahead of time and use a content calendar.

Be authentic and sincere: In managing social media, authenticity and sincerity are essential. Be sincere in your communications with your audience, reply to messages and comments promptly, and manage any issues or concerns forthrightly. For long-term success, you must develop trust with your audience.

Engage audiences: Engage your audience openly on social media since this is what it's there for. Encourage interaction by replying to comments, messages, and mentions. Run surveys, polls, and competitions to promote engagement and build a sense of community.

Monitor and show care: Keep an eye out for conversations about your company and industry on social media. Pay attention to all comments, both positive and negative, and reply promptly and courteously. Utilize customer feedback as a way to grow, learn, and demonstrate your dedication to ensuring their satisfaction.

Optimize visual content: In managing social media, visuals are a powerful tool. To catch audience attention and effectively convey your messages, use high-quality images, videos, infographics, and other visual content. To ensure proper presentation on each social media site, optimize the visuals.

Be consistent: Ensure that your branding is consistent across all of your social media outlets. To establish a unified brand identity, use consistent brand messaging, tone of voice, and images. Your brand's entire image and principles should be reflected in your social media presence.

Stay updated: Maintain up-to-date knowledge of the most recent trends, features, and best practices in social media. To stay relevant and effective, experiment with various content forms, keep up with platform advancements, and modify your strategy as desired.

Evaluate outcomes: Utilize analytics and monitoring tools to evaluate the success of your social media marketing efforts. Keep track of important data such as ROI, reach, impressions, and conversions. To acquire insights, pinpoint problem areas, and improve your plans, analyze the data.

Case 3.3 Leveraging Social Media for Fan Engagement: The Case of FC Barcelona

In the world of sports, effective social media management plays a pivotal role in engaging fans and building a global brand. One illustrative case, for observation, is FC Barcelona, a prestigious football club based in Spain. Applying practical guidelines, the club can be observed successfully connecting with its worldwide fan base, showcasing the power of social media in sports.

Defining Clear Objectives: FC Barcelona exhibits a clear alignment between their social media efforts and overarching objectives. Their observed goals included enhancing fan engagement, increasing brand recognition, and fostering supporters sense of community.

Understanding the Global Audience: The club can be observed carefully identifying its diverse global fan base. Through comprehensive market research, they grasp the preferences, behaviors, and interests of fans from various cultures, tailoring their content accordingly.

Strategizing Content Creation: FC Barcelona develops a comprehensive content strategy. Their plan encompassed diverse content types, from match highlights and player interviews to behind-the-scenes glimpses. This strategy ensured a consistent stream of engaging content, catering to a range of fan interests.

Authentic Interaction: Authenticity is the core feature of FC Barcelona's social media approach. The club demonstrated sincerity by responding promptly to comments, addressing concerns, and fostering open conversations. This cultivates a strong bond of trust and loyalty.

Driving Engagement and Community Building: FC Barcelona actively engage their fans through interactive initiatives. They conduct polls, contests, and quizzes, encouraging fans to participate and connect. This engagement fostered a vibrant online community, enhancing the sense of belonging among supporters.

Monitoring and Customer Care: The club monitors conversations about their team. They respond to both positive and negative comments, showcasing a commitment to fan satisfaction. This attentive approach demonstrates their dedication to listening and adapting.

Leveraging Visual Appeal: Visual content played a significant role in FC Barcelona's social media strategy. High-quality images, videos, and graphics showcased the team's spirit and electrifying moments on the field, captivating fans' attention and enhancing engagement.

Consistency in Branding: Maintaining brand consistency was a priority for FC Barcelona. Their messaging, tone, and imagery remained uniform across various social media platforms, reinforcing their brand identity and values.

Staying Informed and Adapting: FC Barcelona embraced innovation, keeping abreast of social media trends and platform advancements. They experimented with new content formats, staying ahead of the curve and continuously refining their strategy.

Analyzing and Optimizing: It is expected that the club utilizes analytics to measure the success of their social media efforts. They could track metrics such as engagement rates, reach, and conversions, gaining insights to fine-tune their approach and achieve optimal results.

FC Barcelona's experience exemplifies how a sports team should engage a global fan base, enhance brand recognition, and foster community spirit through strategic management.

References

Abeza, G., O'Reilly, N., Seguin, B., & Nzindukiyimana, O. (2017). Social media as a relationship marketing tool in professional sport: A netnographical exploration. *International Journal of Sport Communication, 10*(3), 325–358.

Braunstein-Minkove, J., Insel, A., & Abeza, G. (2021). A Practical Guide to Social Media Management in Sport. In Abeza, G., O'Reilly, N., Sanderson, J., & Fredrick, E. (Eds.). *Social Media in Sport: Theory and Practice*. Barcelona, Spain: World Scientific.

Eberl, N. (2015). *How Content Marketing Helped the All Blacks Win Their Second World Cup in a Row*. www.linkedin.com/pulse/how-content-marketing-helped-all-blacks-win-second-dr-nikolaus/

4 Social Media and Traditional Media

Thus far this book has outlined the numerous ways social media can be used in the marketing and management of sport. It has provided a brief history and basic outline for how social media has developed, the platforms that can be used, and how important social media can be. More to the point, social media platforms have become a nearly compulsory aspect for the communication, interpretation, and promotion of sport from the individual and local recreational level through club and high school, intercollegiate, and professional ranks. Social media has provided space for a multitude of individuals from various backgrounds to post schedules, make instantaneous changes, allow for live scoring and commentary, and even recordings of athletic "feats" performed by, well, almost anyone.

The oft-repeated adage that "anyone can post on social media, all you need is a phone" (Silver et al., 2019) certainly speaks to the democratization of what counts as news or noteworthy. Yet, as the COVID-19 pandemic made clear, not everyone has access to a phone, computer, or reliable Internet nor has the desire to actually use those things to communicate with others (McClain et al., 2021). This means that the population who has access to and makes use of social media, while growing, is still not entirely representative of the global population. Moreover, in some locales, the state government places limits or bans on who can use social media and when. Case in point, France recently banned the use of TikTok, X, and other social media platforms on government phones (Tongo, 2023), and China, Iran, North Korea, Uganda, and Russia do not allow access to Facebook and X (Barry, 2022). In the United States, Utah just banned minors from utilizing social media without parental consent (Singh, 2023).

What this means is that while social media has certainly broadened the population who can have access to and the privilege of (re)presenting modern life via social media, there is still a relatively small subset of the global population that does so with the ability to reach a large audience. As such, the balance of this chapter will provide a more expanded description of the history of media, using its development in the United States as an example, in such a way as to demonstrate the impressive scale and scope of media communications via social media, as well as the relative immediacy with which

DOI: 10.4324/9781003358398-4

it has happened. In so doing, it will outline the changing faces of who gets to report and interpret sports and physical activity. Then it describes the changing forms of social media and breaks down what modern sports television, radio, and social media context looks like. Next, it will expand the focus on social media in sport by providing five global cases for how sport managers, clubs, and media entities have used social media to promote, distribute, communicate, and cover sport. Finally, the chapter concludes by considering possibilities for the future of social and sport media.

Sport and Media

Wilford (2002) suggests that while there is some disagreement over the exact dates when creativity, communication, and language coalesced for *homo sapiens* to roughly resemble what we have become today, there is evidence that human beings have been on earth for roughly 40,000–130,000 years. It was at this time that communication was largely word of mouth and developed into smoke signals in North American tribes and in Ancient China as population spread began to take hold. Cave art began to appear about 35,000 years ago. However, it would be approximately 30,000 years later when the written word and recorded human history began.

During that time, organized, hierarchical structures and attendant inequities were fully developed in the global population (Dubreuil, 2010). To wit, those who could communicate via reading and writing rather than pictures or carvings were limited to those affiliated with a religious community and/or royalty (Kyle, 2014). Even as newer, more accessible forms of mass communication such as the printing press, telegraph, radio, film, television, and satellite communications came to the fore over the last 300 years, the dividing lines between who had access and education to participate in various forms of media communication persisted (see chapter 6).

[Graphic Detailing the History of Human Communication]

The ability to communicate, who is doing the communicating, with whom, and how has been radically altered in the relative blink of an eye, and it is difficult to make sense of what it has meant. One thread that has remained constant throughout the shifting mediascape is that sporting contests, semi-organized physical activity, interpretations, discussions, and arguments (Guttman, 1978) have been key features in the rise of media in general and social media in particular. Indeed, sport and games have been depicted in media dating back to the Ancient Near East, Greek sport, and Roman Empire (Kyle, 2014; Miller, 2004). The fact that these contests and spectacles have been deemed important enough to be recorded throughout time set the tone for the rise of the sports media in more modern times.

For example, in the United States, in the 1820s newspapers and specialty magazines covered things like boxing and horse racing, which allowed a more educated populace to read stories of their favorite fighters and racers (Raney & Bryant, 2009). By the late 1880s the first dedicated sport department was created for *The New York World*, and shortly thereafter the *New York Journal* introduced the first sport section (Rowe, 2007). From there, coverage of sport expanded rather quickly in more standard forms of media such as magazines, newspapers, and radio reports. Scholars have written at length about the development, power, and reach of sports media to communicate major happenings surrounding global spectacles from boxing matches to the Olympics to the World Cup (Tomlinson & Young, 2006).

Live sports radio coverage began in 1921 when KDKA broadcast a boxing match between Johnny Dundee and Johnny Ray to a limited audience. A few months later, Tex Rickard put together a title fight between Jack Dempsey and Georges Carpentier in Jersey City in front of 90,000 fans and broadcast over the radio that reached an area of 125,000 square miles between Maine, Maryland, and Ohio (Bechtel, 2021). Baseball went out over the airwaves in 1921, and other sports soon followed suit. Later, through the use of telephone lines, radio broadcasts were able to reach national audiences, culminating in "the Fight of the Century" between Max Schmeling and Joe Louis in 1938 that an estimated 70 million people listened to over the radio. Louis's win in the rematch against Schmeling made him a national hero in the United States, and he became the first black American sports hero (NPR, 2006).

The advent of the televisual age meant corporate broadcasters needed relatively cheap (and ultimately profitable) programming. Sport, with its built-in narratives, innate competitiveness, and awe-inducing physicality, fit the bill better than any other form of entertainment. So much so, that by 1979 the Entertainment and Sports Programming Network (ESPN) began airing on cable television and has become so profitable in the subsequent 45 years that its parent company (Disney) views it more as a "partner rather than a subsidiary" (Skipper & Samson, 2023). ESPN regularly competes with major broadcast channels CBS, ABS, NBC, and FOX for media rights to major global and U.S. sporting events, and during the dawn of the Internet era, it slowly overtook CBS Sports as the leading voice in online sport media coverage (Miller & Shales, 2011)

Changing Norms: Who Is Doing the (Re)Presenting in the Media

Early in the modern sport media age, the face of the writer, reporter, radio, and televisual personality was overwhelmingly white, heterosexual, and male. What this meant was that for over a century nearly all the interpretive lenses, journalistic interviews, reporting styles, and the like were inflected with white, masculine, heterosexual histories and sensibilities. Occasionally, there were sport journalists who held progressive beliefs and/or wrote and presented about minority athletes, but largely, the sports media landscape remained a bastion of whiteness (Dyer, 1997). Consumers, dialectically informed by their own life histories in relation to those that were being reported to them through sport, have maintained a fairly conservative viewpoint that sports should remain a "male preserve," promoted pro-management opinions about labor strife, and generally valued men's sports over women's.

Case 4.1 Social Media and Sport in Latin America

According to a study by the OmnicomMediaGroup (OMG), the 2012 Olympic Games in London was a watershed moment for social media usage amongst Latin American consumers of sporting content (Gonzalez, 2013). Though, at the time, television remained the primary source for these individuals to engage with sports, Facebook, X, and YouTube began making major strides against terrestrial television. The OMG study found that this was the case, because consumers wanted round-the-clock and real-time engagement with the Olympics, and this sport media consumption pattern increased in the ensuing years.

Today, millions of unique sport media users from the "six largest markets in Latin America – Argentina, Brazil, Chile, Mexico, Colombia, and Peru" (Guttman, 2023) engage with sports on a daily basis. In these countries, soccer/futbol sites AS, ESPN, DEPOR, and Marca generate between 25.7 and 37.5 million users. Certainly, soccer/futbol is a chief driver of social media content and engagement, but sites such as AS, ESPN, TNT, and DAZN provide coverage and the ability for consumers to interact with a variety of sporting content. All told, social media has become a major factor in Latin American sport media.

Sources: https://espnpressroom.com/us/press-releases/2013/02/omnicommediagroup-and-espn-international-study-reveals-that-latin-american-sports-fans-consume-sports-on-more-devices-than-ever-use-social-media-for-sports-iformation/amp/

www.statista.com/statistics/1184692/sports-media-unique-users-latin-america/

What Does This Look Like Now and in the Future

The social media age has most certainly had a major impact on the ways that sport media content is produced. Magazines such as *Sports Illustrated*, once a pillar in the sport media industry, have all but collapsed as their production takes far too long for the modern-day consumer. The entertainment aspect of sport media introduced in television has shaped not only the televisual programming context but all sport media communications. Furthermore, the niche elements of sport consumers and production of sport content insofar as anyone with a smartphone and an Internet connection can produce consumables has taken over. If one were to seek out progressive (even academically) based sport information on things such as blogs, podcasts, YouTube, X, and so forth, they can – just as someone can curate their own feeds to only receive more traditional conservative-based programming (King-White, 2023). This section seeks to outline what the modern sport media landscape looks like.

Case 4.2   Tencent and Chinese Sport Social Media

The State Council of China released a document in 2014 that detailed a plan to raise consumption of sport via social media platforms dramatically over the course of the ensuing decade, and led to a "boom" in online sport media creation and consumption (Daxueconsulting, 2019). As the number of online sport media consumers in China grew from 80 million in 2012 to 410 million in 2016, several companies sought to engage with this developing state-sponsored growth market – namely, Sina Sports, Alibaba Group, and Tencent Sports. Although all three have experienced some level of success, the latter has matured in the social media market the quickest.

In 2014, Tencent Sports purchased the rights to stream NBA broadcasts to pair with and drive consumption of its online NBA game. Soon thereafter they purchased the rights to the English Premier League (EPL), National Hockey League (NHL), and became "the most popular Chinese online sports media platform" (Daxuconsulting, 2019). However, the broadcast rights to sports became cost prohibitive, and Tencent later negotiated with ESPN to share rights and channels with one another. This has proven useful to Tencent, as they have been able to effectively compete with the more established and traditional Sina Sports media company to become the leading social media platform for sports in China.

Source: https://daxueconsulting.com/chinese-online-sports-media-platforms/

Sport Television

For years many spoke of "cord cutting" and getting rid of their cable and local television packages to move toward a more streaming media environment. Indeed, the number of subscribers to cable television has plummeted by almost 10 million subscribers in the last few years (Huston, 2023). Regional cable channels that used things like baseball as cheap programming filler during the slow summer months have also collapsed (outside of the New York Yankees and Boston Red Sox channels), leaving several teams in a state of financial instability

(Gonzalez, 2023). COVID-19 also hurt (sports) television since, for a short period, there were no games to watch, and people found solace in actually participating in sport themselves (King-White & Giardina, forthcoming). Though non-sports viewers have largely stayed away from television in favor of streaming options, live sport programming remains vital in the modern sport media environment for major national programmers ESPN, FOX, NBC, and CBS.

Radio

As was mentioned previously, sports on the radio began in the early 1920s with the first boxing match, as well as baseball and football games being announced over the airwaves. With relatively limited reach compared to television, announcers became the voice for local teams and gained fame and loyal followings. Yet, and perhaps in the first glimpses of what social media would look like, sports commentary radio began in 1964 with Bill Mazer, who took phone calls on Brooklyn-based WNBC (Goldstein, 2013). The dialogue between everyday people and radio personalities birthed a new feature in sports media that heretofore was left to "letters to the editor," and it caught on. So much so, that when *Mike and the Mad Dog* (Mike Francesca and Christopher "Mad Dog" Russo) were paired on WFAN radio in New York in 1989, an entire generation of passionate, argument-based sports conversation on the radio exploded for listeners' entertainment and influenced modern sports radio broadcasting at the present moment. The regional reach of sports radio means that local voices speak to the unique cultures of the towns they represent, with Boston's WEEI and The Sports Hub often bespeaking a virulent form of white masculinity and racism that fits with both the town and traditional media voices, as compared to The Fan in Baltimore being more diverse from a socio-political perspective (Spearman, 2021). Again, while the AM radio frequency slowly fades in favor of satellite and FM options, sports still holds a space for loyal listeners.

Internet and Blogs

The Internet served as a new frontier for sports content. No longer did consumers have to wait overnight or weeks to get their sports news; rather, scores were updated live as they happened. It became possible to know what was happening, when it was happening, no matter where it was happening. Therefore, the need for magazines and newspapers began to wane, and in their stead arose ESPN.com and CBSsportsline.com. For the first few years in the Internet era, both competed for clicks and advertisement revenue by hiring writers and columnists away from newspapers and magazines and having them write stories and opinions for a national audience. For a time, CBS was the most revered sports-based website, but under then-President John Skipper's direction, ESPN slowly took over.

Skipper brought in a diversity of voices, bloggers, and even Hunter S. Thompson in an attempt to reach more people from a variety of backgrounds – and it worked. Most notably, Bill Simmons, who had his own *Boston Sports Guy* blog, parlayed his Boston (Red Sox) "homer" viewpoint blended with (now very dated) popular culture references in a way that really connected with readers, who either liked or hated his material. In many ways his work borrowed from Mike and the Mad Dog's argumentative and semi-controversial stylings and put it to print. Simmons would go on to have a major creative influence and/or direction over numerous things like the *ESPN 30 for 30* sports documentary series, his own podcast, and even, for a brief moment, a show on *HBO*. Eventually, his bombastic styling and success led to a parting from ESPN, where he built his own media company The Ringer.

Academic and pseudo-academic blogs such as the Maryland-based *The Corpus* and *Edge of Sports* and sports politics *Politico* allowed for a more critical viewpoint on sport and amassed a relatively popular following. Others, seeing Simmons' success by starting as a blogger who was not viewed as a particularly skillful writer within the sport journalist community (c.f. Burneko, 2015), thought that they could blend sport and social media better than him. For instance, up-and-coming journalists wrote local stories for *Bleacher Report*, comedic reviews of sports came from blogs such as *Kissing Suzy Kolber*, and *Fire Joe Morgan* featuring the stylings of authors who worked for places and shows like *Saturday Night Live*, *The Office*, and *Parks and Recreation*. However, the two most popular sites to emerge from the blogging industry were *Deadspin* and *Barstool*.

Early on, both of these blogs mixed crass, hypermasculine, and sexualized content with sports commentary. Most notably, the story of Brett Favre's alleged sexual harassment of Jen Sterger and other New York Jets employees was broken (with photographs) by *Deadspin*, which served to put it on the maps of various consumers (Smith, 2022). However, as *Deadspin* evolved and hired a more diverse cast of writers who covered politics, sexuality, gender, racial, and class privilege on a variety of sporting topics, it became a left-leaning source of sport information. Drew Magary often gets the highest billing, and numerous other talented writers from the site such as Lauren Thiessen and Laura Wagner are recognizable (amongst many, many others); perhaps the best example of the political and topical diversity on *Deadspin* was David Roth's coverage of Donald Trump's presidency. *Deadspin* eventually became embroiled in a legal dispute (covered in Chapter 5), and the writers, unhappy with new ownership directives, eventually broke off to form their own company *Defector*.

Converse to *Deadspin/Defector*, *Barstool* never chose to evolve. Led by David Portnoy, who has been accused of sexual misconduct by multiple women (Madani, 2021) and the general mistreatment of his employees, the company profits off the traditional hypermasculine consumer of sports (Leitch, 2018). Those who do not value diversity, enjoy the sexualization of women, and have a general "men will be men" attitude tend to flock to *Barstool*. Indeed, barstool stickers are ubiquitous on the laptops of college students and the bumper stickers of cars, and flags carrying the moniker "Saturdays are for the Boys" reign supreme for those who prefer the traditional sport mediascape and Make America Great Again viewpoint (Garzia & Proffitt, 2022; Kusz & Hodler, 2022).

Importantly, both of these companies were able to amass loyal followings based on the ways they were able to borrow from and expand on sports talk radio's ability to allow consumers to engage with producers of content. Indeed, some of the most loyal readers of weblogs are those who registered for a handle and post responses to articles and video content posted on blogs. Sometimes the commenters are even hired to write articles and become blogger personalities for websites, and as other social media platforms like X arose, the arguments, humor, and back and forth birthed from this content migrated there. Some who ally with *Deadspin/Defector* choose to engage with content on *Barstool* "hate read" and post on the rival site and vice versa (Baker, 2012).

Case 4.3 Social Media and Sport in Africa

Africa is considered to be a developing frontier for social media content consumption. This is because a large portion of the continent's population does not have access to smartphones, the Internet, and/or television. In 2022 only 40% of the population had a mobile phone, and that number is expected to hit 50% by 2025 (Pinetown, 2022). Given such relatively meager market saturation, Africa is a potentially lucrative market for sporting social media content producers. Furthermore, doing this through social media has become imperative as consumers with smartphone and Internet technology actually outnumber those households that own a single television, and that difference in the number of consumers with a phone and television is expected to widen considerably in the coming years (Silver et al., 2019).

In Africa one of the biggest challenges has been how to best monetize broadcasts for the NBA-organized Basketball Africa League (BAL), as well as other forms of domestic and international sport programming. Mobile providers have worked through some murky banking options to simply add the costs of engaging with such sport programming to the consumers' phone bill. The unique nature of African consumers being considered "mobile first" means that as the portion of the population with smartphones grows, so does the potential for social media reach a profitability for content creators.

Sources: www.sportspromedia.com/opinions/sports-ott-mobile-streaming-africa-mnos-pm-connect/?zephr_sso_ott=kAP2o7

www.statista.com/statistics/249626/pay-tv-penetration-in-sub-saharan-africa/

Podcasts

Interestingly, but not shockingly, not every consumer likes to read and not every sports content producer likes to write. Mirroring the cord-cutting related to appointment television and the on-demand nature of modern life rendering "drive time" sports radio a bit of an anachronism, podcasting has become an increasingly important aspect of the sports media landscape. Mentioned previously, Bill Simmons left ESPN to create his own media company that features several podcasts for The Ringer. In addition, *Deadspin/Defector* and *Barstool* also have birthed podcasts where they interact with athletes and other celebrities and are able to be recorded, cleaned up, and made available for download whenever anyone has the time to listen to them.

Many of ESPN's top on-air talents such as Domonique Foxworth, Bomani Jones, Sarah Spain, Mina Kimes, and more have used the company's infrastructure to produce and post their own podcasts that allows them to break free of the requirements of traditional sports radio in that, yes, there are commercials, but recordings are not reduced to fitting into set segments. Some podcasts can last 20 minutes and others can go for hours. Athletes such as Pat McAfee and Draymond Green have gotten into the fray as well, realizing they are no longer required to speak to journalists when their own voices have value for consumers and do not need to be guided or interpreted through the lens of others who may or, as is often the case, may not share their values and viewpoints.

However, perhaps the most high-profile example of this in relation to the chapter as written has been Dan LeBatard. Hired away from the *Miami Herald* to ESPN by John Skipper as a means of drawing on his distinctly Latin Cuban-American worldview to create his own television show with Bomani Jones (*Highly Questionable*), LeBatard also brought his radio show *The Dan LeBatard Show with Stugotz* and its rabidly loyal following to ESPN Radio. The latter gained in national popularity after its celebration of the local Miami Heat's signing of LeBron James, and never looked back. Eventually, LeBatard became disaffected by ESPN following Skipper's resignation from the company and its turn away from political speech during the Trump presidency. He was suspended, some might even say disavowed, by the company after giving an impassioned speech about one of Trump's many controversial political decisions, and a show producer was eventually let go by ESPN in a cost-saving measure.

LeBatard would eventually leave ESPN with his radio show talent and team back up with John Skipper to form Meadowlark Media; he signed a $50 million contract with *Draft Kings* to produce their radio show in podcast form along with content across numerous foci. His co-host, John "Stugotz" Weiner, and one of the show's producers, Billy Gil, have created an extremely popular podcast *God Bless Football*; another producer helped create a musical *The Big Game*; and other producers and contributors to the show have podcasts ranging from women's sport (*Off the Looking Glass*), sport journalism (*Meadowlarkers*), film (*Cinephile* and *Cinephobe*), comedy (*The Jim Brockmire Show*), and even produced a film (*The Good Rivals*), to name just a few. In addition to gathering talented producers and on-air talent, *Meadowlark* has siphoned the likes of Amin el-Hassan, Kate Fagan, Howard Bryant, Pablo Torre, Adnan Virk, David Samson, Rene Montgomery, Spencer Hall, and more from ESPN to its platform to create their own content and/or participate in the show as well. In many ways, *Meadowlark* is the best example to date of the shift away from the traditional media landscape towards one where consumers can reach out and connect with the company through social media such as X, Reddit, and YouTube.

Social (Sport) Media From a Global Perspective

The United States provides a good primer for tracing the development of sport media and its relationship to and with social media. However, it is but one example of how social media has become intertwined with the promotion and coverage of sport. Globally speaking, social media has become a major part of growth strategies for teams, leagues, and individuals. These approaches range from obtaining broadcasting rights to live events, fan engagement, revenue generation, traditional media coverage, and (youth) league development. Throughout this chapter are five examples for how this has taken shape in the contemporary moment. To be sure, this is not an exhaustive list, but rather a few interesting instances that show how social media has become an integral part of global sport media.

Case 4.4   Social Media Trends for Soccer Clubs in Europe

Europe is different from some of the other cases presented in this chapter in that the social media market tends to be much more developed and mature. What this means is that the market for users who engage with soccer/futbol clubs in Europe via social media platforms like Instagram and Facebook has become nearly saturated. Top clubs Juventus, Real Madrid, FC Barcelona, and Manchester United boast users on both platforms that range from 50–110 million, and though this ability to reach consumers for merchandising and sponsorship revenue is large, capitalism requires constant growth.

Enter TikTok. The online video-sharing application allows for users to create and share short videos demonstrating their fandom, connecting with others, and just pure entertainment. Though they lag behind the big three (Madrid, Barcelona, and Man United) when it comes to the more traditional social media platforms like Facebook and Instagram, Paris Saint-Germain (PSG) far outstrips all other clubs when it comes to TikTok engagement, with nearly 25 million followers (double their nearest competitors). Though their recent loss of global superstar Lionel Messi to Miami FC may prove damaging, PSG is well-positioned to take advantage of TikTok's developing popularity in the face of the stagnating nature of Facebook and Instagram (Jahns, 2022).

Source: www.ispo.com/en/markets/soccer-clubs-europes-top-10-social-media

Future of Social Media in Sport Industry

When taking into account the growth and development of the (sport) media landscape, it is breathtaking how quickly it has changed. Put differently, if we can conservatively suggest that recorded human history is 30,000 years, it has really been in the last 20 years, or .06% of that time, that social media has existed. Yet, it has become the norm with which people communicate, promote, sell, and consume sport. So much so, that it would be odd to live in a world where social media did not dominate the ways we experience sport from youth to professional ranks. Furthermore, it allows for more information and more content to be shared in a multitude of formats that best reach the niche consumption patterns of sport enthusiasts.

Case 4.5 The Junior Tour Powered by UnderArmour

The Junior Tour Powered by Under Armour (UAJT) began as a junior golf competition in 2020 based primarily in Florida, Maryland, and Illinois. Junior golf in the United States is a surprisingly crowded marked, with Notah Begay III, Optimist, USGA Amateur, Buckeye, Hurricane, Callaway, and U.S. Kids, among others (including local city and county tours) offering competitions. As a latecomer to the scene and opening up during COVID-19, the UAJT had several obstacles to overcome. Still they grew slowly over the past few years by utilizing social media sites and applications such as Facebook, SportsEngine, and Golf Genius to communicate information about leagues and events as well as tee times and scores for participants. When league franchises started to spread from the original 5 to nearly 50 in 21 different states across the country, UAJT director Ray Taranto hired Olga Diaz to become the Vice President of Media Relations. Diaz had experience in event sales, communications, and promotions and took to social media in order to promote the UAJT:

> YouTube: Diaz put her promotions expertise in action by starting the UAJT YouTube channel. She sent out a mass text message and email to parents asking them to record their kids playing in hopes that they could catch an incredible shot or moment during a tournament.

She turned those into weekly Top 9 shots of the week packages, interviewed some of the top players on the tour, and cut them down into 10-minute informational interviews about how the kids hoped to use golf in their lives. In addition, she provided overall and age-group-specific recaps for National and World Championship events that the UAJT held throughout 2022.

X: Local UAJT franchises use the application to promote their existence and reach parents and participants.

Instagram: Locally and nationally, the UAJT has a presence on Instagram to share and communicate information about National and World Championships, as well as links to YouTube videos posted by Diaz.

Facebook: League directors and Taranto use their individual and league Facebook pages to share top shots and moments during events, and to spread information about upcoming opportunities to sign up for league play.

With its blend of professionally packaged and uniquely local social media promotions, the UAJT has amassed the largest social media following in junior golf programming within a year. By being at the forefront of utilizing social media, the UAJT has been able to surpass many other more established leagues to reach more consumers, and by using the citizen journalist to effectively outsource videography, has been able to help generate further interest in the service of the UAJT.

Looking ahead, it seems clear that as the terrestrial television user ages out and the cord-cutting younger generation becomes the norm, more and more options for streaming will become available. This will require even faster and more responsive streaming times as Amazon, Apple TV, Netflix, YouTube, and Yahoo! start to bid for and even win the rights fees to cover major sporting events. It also means that more and more families who live in disparate areas can share their (children's) sporting experiences from the youth and amateur levels that were not available prior to more recent times.

However, there is concern that there may be some level of sport "information overload of the same sport, mainly about male professional leagues and big international mega-events, while lower leagues, youth competitions and women's games are excluded" (Ramon & Rojas-Torrijos, 2022, p. 923). With so many options and brands to choose from that have a variety of strengths, weaknesses, overarching political affiliations (or at least the perception of it), as well as changing preferences amongst consumers, it remains to be seen which television channels, blogs, websites, podcasts, and streaming options will rise to the top as others fall by the wayside. Regardless, there is no doubt that the changes social media has brought about within the sport media landscape are here to stay.

References

Baker, K. (2012). The art of hate-reading. *Jezebel.* https://jezebel.com/the-art-of-hate-reading-5876891

Barry, E. (2022). These are countries where Twitter, Facebook and TikTok are banned. *Time.* Accessed March 31, 2023 from https://time.com/6139988/countries-where-twitter-facebook-tiktok-banned/

Bechtel, M. (2021). How boxing launched radio. *Sports Illustrated.* Accessed March 31, 2023 from https://www.si.com/boxing/2021/06/30/how-boxing-launched-radio-daily-cover

Blackley, S. (2016). History of communication timeline. *Prezi.* Accessed October 13, 2023 from https://prezi.com/cz2e34xjsyd_/history-of-communication-timeline/

Burneko, A. (2015). Bill Simmons is a shitty writer. *Deadspin.* https://deadspin.com/bill-simmons-is-a-shitty-writer-1703163076.

daxuconsulting. (2019). *The Chinese Online Sports Market.* https://daxueconsulting.com/chinese-online-sports-media-platforms/.

Dubreuil, B. (2010). *Human evolution and the origins of hierarchies: The State of nature.* New York: Cambridge University Press.

Dyer, R. (1997). *White: Essays on race and culture.* London: Routledge.

Garcia, C., & Proffitt, J. (2022). Recontextualizing Barstool sports and misogyny in online US sports media. *Communication & Sport, 10*(4), 730–745.

Goldstein, R. (2013). Bill Mazer, sports fixture in New York, dies at 92. *The New York Times.* Accessed March 31, 2023 from https://www.nytimes.com/2013/10/24/sports/bill-mazer-a-sports-fixture-of-new-york-radio-and-tv-dies-at-92.html

Gonzalez, J. (2013). OmnicomMediaGroup and ESPN International study reveals that Latin American sports fans consume sports on more devices than ever, use social media for sports information. *ESPN Press Room.* https://espnpressroom.com/us/press-releases/2013/02/omnicommediagroup-and-espn-international-study-reveals-that-latin-american-sports-fans-consume-sports-on-more-devices-than-ever-use-social-media-for-sports-information/?noamp=mobile

Gonzalez, A. (2013). What the RSN mess means for MLB on TV, future of blackouts. *ESPN.* https://www.espn.com/mlb/story/_/id/35864012/rsns-diamond-sports-group-bankruptcy-bally-blackouts-mlb-tv

Guttman, A. (1978). *From ritual to record: The Nature of modern sports.* New York: Columbia University Press.

Huston, C. (2023). Pay TV and cable providers lost 5.8M subscribers in 2022. *The Hollywood Reporter.* Accessed March 31, 2023 from https://www.hollywoodreporter.com/business/business-news/cord-cutting-2022-cable-pay-subscriber-losses-1235340253/

Jahns, M. (2022). *Soccer Clubs: Europe's Top 10 on Social Media 2022.* www.ispo.com/en/markets/soccer-clubs-europes-top-10-social-media

King-White, R. (2023). Social media scholarship in sport studies and the state of cultural studies. *International Journal of Sport Communication, 16*(3), 366–371.

King-White, R., & Giardina, M. (2023). Parenting in pandemic times: Notes on the emotional geography of youth sport culture. In. D. Andrews, H. Thorpe & J. Newman (Eds.) *Sport and Physical Culture in Global Pandemic Times: COVID Assemblages* (pp. 445–469). Cham: Springer International Publishing.

Kusz, K., & Hodler, M. (2022). "Saturdays are for the boys": Barstool sports and the cultural politics of white fratriarchy in contemporary America. *Sociology of Sport Journal, 40*(1), 96–107.

Kyle, D. (2014). *Sport and spectacle in the ancient world*. Malden, MA: John Wiley & Sons, Inc.

Leitch, W. (2018). What fresh hell is Barstool sports? *Intelligencer*. https://nymag.com/intelligencer/2018/09/what-fresh-kind-of-hell-is-barstool-sports.html

Madani, D. (2021). Barstool sports' Dave Portnoy denies sexual misconduct allegations. *NBC News*. www.nbcnews.com/news/us-news/barstool-sports-dave-portnoy-denies-sexual-misconduct-allegations-rcna4609

McClain, C., Vogels, E., Perrin, A., Sechopoulous, S., & Ranie, L. (2021). The Internet and the pandemic. *Pew Research Center*. Accessed March 31, 2023 from https://www.pewresearch.org/internet/2021/09/01/the-internet-and-the-pandemic/

Miller, S. (2004). *Ancient Greek athletics*. New Haven, CT: Yale University Press.

Miller, J., & Shales, T. (2011). *Those guys have all the fun: Inside the world of ESPN*. New York: Little, Brown and Company.

NPR. (2006). *All things considered*. Accessed March 31, 2023 from https://www.npr.org/2006/11/25/6515548/the-fight-of-the-century-louis-vs-schmeling

Pinetown, D. (2022). *Africa is the New Frontier for Sports OTT and Mobile is the Gateway*. www.sportspromedia.com/opinions/sports-ott-mobile-streaming-africa-mnos-pm-connect/?zephr_sso_ott=kAP2o7

Ramon, X., & Rojas-Torrijos, J. (2022). Public service media, sports and cultural citizenship in the age of social media: An analysis of BBC Sport agenda diversity on Twitter. *International Review for the Sociology of Sport*, 57(6), 918–939.

Raney, A., & Bryant, J. (2009). *Handbook of sports and media*. London: Routledge.

Rowe, D. (2007). Sports journalism: Still the toy department of the news media? *Journalism*, 8(4), 395–405.

Silver, L., Smith, A., Johnson, C., Jiang, J., Anderson, M., & Ranie, L. (2019). Mobile connectivity in emerging economies. *Pew Research Center*. Accessed March 31, 2023 from https://www.pewresearch.org/internet/2019/03/07/use-of-smartphones-and-social-media-is-common-across-most-emerging-economies/

Singh, M. (2023). Utah bans under-18s from using social media unless parents consent. *The Guardian*. Accessed March 31, 2023 from https://www.theguardian.com/us-news/2023/mar/23/utah-social-media-access-law-minors

Skipper, J., & Samson, D. (2023). Sports business with John Skipper and David Samson. *The Dan LeBatard Show 3/1/2023*. Accessed March 31, 2023 from https://www.youtube.com/watch?v=-udD5zUcvD0

Smith, C. (2022). Brett Favre was a sexually harassing creep long before (allegedly) robbing Mississippi's poor. *Daily Beast*. https://news.yahoo.com/brett-favre-sexually-harassing-creep-085751219.html?fr=yhssrp_catchall

Spearman, L. (2021). Low hanging fruit: How sports talk radio hosts discuss racism. *Communication & Sport*, 9(6), 934–953.

Tomlinson, A., & Young, C. (Eds.) (2006). *National identity and global sports events: Culture, politics and spectacle in the Olympics and the Football World Cup*. Albany, NY: SUNY Press.

Tongo, R. (2023). France bans 'recreational' use of TikTok, Twitter, Instagram. *Aljazeera*. Accessed March 31, 2023 from https://www.aljazeera.com/news/2023/3/25/france-bans-tiktok-on-work-phones-of-civil-servants

Wilford, J. (2002). When humans became human. *The New York Times*. Accessed March 31, 2023 from https://www.nytimes.com/2002/02/26/science/when-humans-became-human.html

5 Social Media and Legal and Ethical Issues

Social media has many wonderful aspects in that it allows people to communicate ideas, messages, and beliefs via audio, photographic, and video images in ways never before possible. For parents and coaches of youth and amateur sports, social media has helped provide space for scheduling, feedback, and the creation of "highlight packages" that can be sent to college recruiters across the United States (Bustad & Mower, 2018), or posted on places like YouTube, Instagram, Facebook, and X for family and friends from disparate places around the world to watch their (grand)children, nieces, and nephews celebrate a first hit, magisterial goal, buzzer-beater basket, clutch putt, or simply kick a ball and roll in the grass. As esports develop as a legitimate sporting endeavor, websites and applications such as Twitch allow for live streaming and recording of online games with audio and video feedback from fans.

Put simply, social media has culturally accelerated a society that was already experiencing dramatic shifts via time and space compression (Harvey, 1999). Time/space compression refers to the modern condition whereby humans are able to travel from one place to another more quickly and safely than at any other time in human history and/or transmit cultural ideas, norms, and values instantaneously and in person. For those that value diversity of ideas, people, and culture, this all sounds fantastic. However, it is not always the case that social media produces positive results. Just as social media can provide the space for familial and friend group connectivity, it can also be a source for the transmission of hate speech and sharing of audio and video that crosses moral and ethical barriers that have led to a number of discussions, concerns, and developments in the legal world.

While Chapter 4 outlines the production of and who can produce social media in and around sports, this chapter looks at the consequences of the rise of social media on and off the field from a legal and ethical standpoint. Given the murkiness around what counts as and/or how to police online language, harassment/abuse when the user could simply choose not to engage with the form of media, as well as the risks involved with social media usage from an individual and organizational standpoint, this chapter discusses these issues with regard to social media and free speech, amateur/college athletes and coaches, harassment, abuse, maltreatment, and general legal risks with social media.

Social Media and Free Speech

On December 15, 1791, the United States government ratified Amendment I to the constitution of their government. It reads:

> Congress shall make no law respecting an establishment of religion, or prohibiting the free exercise thereof; or abridging the freedom of speech, or of the press; or the right of the people peaceably to assemble, and to petition the Government for a redress of grievances.
>
> (Bill of Rights Institute, 2023, p. 10)

Those 45 words defending an individual's "right to free speech" have long been challenged, misunderstood, and/or litigated in the country. More to the point, the First Amendment has limitations on obscenity, child pornography, and words that incite violence (a.k.a. "fighting words") (Ruane, 2014, p. 4). So, it can safely be stated that not all speech is free and no speech is free from the consequences of its use.

The Internet and social media, with the faux privacy (Baccarella et al., 2018) afforded by a pixelated screen, have further complicated matters between what constitutes public/private communication on public/private platforms. Users have been able to use social media sites to promote oppositional forms of communication that do not require the same journalistic or peer-reviewed standards as traditional forms of media and academia. This can allow for the development of dangerous political collectives based on the spreading of mythologies and purposeful misinformation. These conspiratorial posts from sources such as QAnon have led to the formation of groups who have questioned the veracity of political elections throughout the world.

Globally, a 2021 report by Freedom House found that there has been a concerted effort to restrict the sharing of "information" on social media platforms. In 2021 "officials in at least 20 countries suspended internet access, and 20 regimes blocked access to social media platforms ... the biggest declines were seen in Myanmar, Belarus, and Uganda" (Paul, 2021, para. 8). Further, China was found to be the most brazen in its attempts to block free speech on social media platforms. Yet, in most countries, social media usage is legal, vast, and very difficult to monitor from a legal standpoint given that users can be from other countries and therefore do not have the same legal responsibilities as a citizen of the country that created the law.

Case 5.1 Japanese Olympic Team and Cyberbullying

During the 2020 Olympics held in Tokyo, Japan, several athletes from the host country realized athletic glory by earning 58 medals (including 27 golds) during the event. However, several athletes in a variety of disciplines such as gymnastics, table tennis, and hurdles were subject to cyberbullying on social media platforms. Some were chastised for seemingly taking advantage of favoritism from judges, while some were harangued for poor performances, and others were exposed to racist posts and comments. What is interesting about this particular case is that the Japanese parliament had proactively established a law meant to dissuade such treatment, and the Japanese Olympic Committee (JOC) monitored accounts to protect athletes from online abuse.

Unfortunately, the global nature of the Olympics meant that most of the inflammatory and racist material was generated from international sources, meaning that the perpetrators could not be held legally responsible for their behavior. For their part, the Japanese parliament strengthened the law against "online insults" to result in up to one year in prison and 300,000 yen ($2200USD), which is a "significant increase from the existing punishments of detention for fewer than 30 days and a fine of up to 10,000 yen ($75USD)" (Yeung et al., 2022), following the suicide of a reality television star related to cyberbullying. This law, however, is complicated for athletes beyond the national source of cyberbullying, because there exists much consternation and disagreement over what constitutes an "insult."

Sources: www.cnn.com/2022/06/14/asia/japan-cyberbullying-law-intl-hnk-scli/index.html

https://english.kyodonews.net/news/2021/07/13be0e90b1a9-olympic-athletes-pained-by-online-bashing-mental-health-care-sought.html

Media Members as Company Representatives

Outside the distinctly political realm, the world of sports has had to contend with a number of issues regarding free speech on social media. Typically, this comes to fruition when a traditional sports media member and/or athlete chooses to use a social media platform in order to share a political opinion, and the reaction by the company they work for is to either suspend or dismiss the worker from the job, leading to a discussion about "freedom of speech" and where it can take place. Two relatively recent examples on opposite sides of the political spectrum in sports are ESPN's Curt Schilling and Jemele Hill.

Curt Schilling

Curt Schilling had an exemplary career as a starting pitcher in Major League Baseball (MLB). He pitched in numerous post-season games for the Philadelphia Phillies, Arizona Diamondbacks, and Boston Red Sox, earning the admiration of many for his clutch performances as part of three different World Series–winning teams (Adler & Kelly, 2022). When Schilling transitioned to his post-playing career, he headed a failed gaming company 38Studios (Moskovitz, 2015), and became a baseball analyst for ESPN, offering pitching and game insights on a variety of show platforms. However, his social media presence was often littered with far-right conservative messaging that did not please his bosses at ESPN (Draper, 2016).

Schilling was warned numerous times to stop posting these messages since not all viewers of ESPN shared his extremely conservative views, and there was concern that this may cost the company sponsors and viewers (Draper, 2016). In April 2016, Schilling posted an "image of a man in a wig with his breasts exposed, captioned, "LET HIM IN! to the restroom with your daughter or else you're a narrow-minded, judgmental, unloving racist bigot who needs to die" (Holloway, 2016), and further commented "A man is a man no matter what they call themselves. I don't care what they are, who they sleep with, men's room was designed for the penis, women's not so much. Now you need laws telling us differently? Pathetic" (Holloway, 2016). Given that this was not the first instance of him posting controversial subject matter and that he had been reprimanded previously, ESPN quickly dismissed Schilling from his position.

Jemele Hill

Jemele Hill is a black female sports journalist who worked for numerous newspapers before ending up at ESPN in 2006. From there, Hill progressed upwardly within the company until she was finally offered a position as a co-host on ESPN2's *Numbers Never Lie*, which later became *His & Hers* and *SC6* (both with Michael Smith as co-host). Outside of a single controversial incident in 2008 regarding fans of the Boston Celtics and race (Heslam, 2008), Hill was known for her exemplary work ethic and progressive stances on race, gender, and sexuality. However, in 2017, a year into Donald Trump's presidency and at the height of the Colin Kaepernick protest, Hill published the following series of posts on X:

"Donald Trump is a white supremacist who has largely surrounded himself w/ other white supremacists" (Hill, 2017a).

"Trump is the most ignorant, offensive president of my lifetime. His rise is a direct result of white supremacy. Period" (Hill, 2017b).

"He has surrounded himself with white supremacists – no they are not "alt right" – and you want me to believe he isn't a white supremacist?" (Hill, 2017c).

"He is unqualified and unfit to be president. He is not a leader. And if he were not white, he never would have been elected" (Hill, 2017d).

It was clear that Hill had been reprimanded but received no outward-facing punishment until she was suspended for two weeks when she posted that fans should boycott the advertisers who support Jerry Jones (team owner) and the Dallas Cowboys after Jones suggested he would "bench anyone who disrespected the flag" (Draper & Belson, 2017).

Each of these situations conjured much consternation across the political sphere, as well as generated questions about what counts as public versus private communication. O'Hallarn et al. (2018) found that much of the discussion was about ESPN not wanting to support free speech and/or pushing a "liberal agenda," while others found that Schilling was bigoted and deserved punishment. Relatedly, those who supported Hill also suggested ESPN did not care about free speech, while others suggested she should be fired for criticizing the President on the Internet (Wallance, 2017; West, 2018).

High School Athletes

Schilling and Hill were employees of the same company and deemed to be representatives given their positions of relevance, which made it easier to sanction their social media posts. High school students generally have more protection given the lack of reach and impact their social media activities can have. This situation gets trickier when amateur athletes at the high school and collegiate levels are involved. More to the point, the U.S. court system has found that participating in voluntary, extracurricular sport is not an essential part of one's education at the high school level (Sawyer et al., 2012). What this means is that student-athletes are generally subject to discipline from coaches and other authority figures related to playing time and/or participation on a team if they directly seek to undermine them via social media postings and sharing of things like petitions to fire their coach in public forums, because it interferes with the administrator's ability to exercise authority in these situations (Lever, 2022).

College Athletes

Collegiate athletes are in a slightly different arena from those in high school. First, nearly all college athletes are legally adults, and their coaches are not viewed as caretakers in the same way as those in high school are. The National Collegiate Athletic Association (NCAA) also purposefully has written into its charter that student-athletes are not to be viewed as employees deserving of direct fiscal compensation, insurance, and liability coverage (Epstein & Anderson, 2015). However, student-athletes are viewed as public-facing representatives of the institution they play for. As social media came into vogue in the early 2010s, many coaches and schools at private and public institutions implemented in-season social media bans for their players, while others did so completely (Umar, 2015).

Private institutions have been able to maintain this practice since they are not considered governmental institutions with the same legal requirements as public (state) schools. However, as social media further infiltrated everyday life, questions about these types of bans have come under fire at public colleges and universities as they are, in the most basic sense, supposed to be a space for the freedom of expression within the marketplace of ideas (Mayer, 2013). Social media bans, in the first instance, run directly counter to this fundamental notion. This was particularly true as student-athletes began organizing to speak for and against participating in intercollegiate athletics during the onset of the COVID-19 pandemic and other political issues like the Black Lives Matter movement (Harrigan, 2020).

Second, as with other legal issues, such as student-athletes' right to earn compensation on their Name Image and Likeness (NIL), in more recent times, these types of bans can actually be seen as a method of undermining student-athletes' means of earning fiscal compensation. Indeed, in a most recent example, Haley and Hanna Cavinder, social media influencers and University of Miami women's basketball players, were not penalized for social media posts depicting an impermissible meal with booster John Ruiz during a time when they were choosing to transfer from Fresno State to Miami (Forde & Dellenger, 2023). Though their coach served a three-game suspension to start the season, this relatively minor punishment is a stark contrast to some of the draconian bans and punishments levied early in the social media era.

Male Preserve

Data shows that the (sport) workplace has become more "feminized" in ways that have upended traditional familial norms and the face of the office (King-White, 2022; King-White & Giardina, 2023). Women have entered the labor market in higher numbers, remained there later in life, and more have earned promotions to positions of power than ever before, but this experience has not proven to be a steady slide of progress and has generated many negative consequences. More to the point, it has been convincingly argued and supported by evidence that sport, in general, is a *male preserve* (Dunning, 1986; Theberge, 1985) that runs counter to the notion that athletics is a space for equal access, participation, and mutual respect. As Dunning and Theberge originally suggested, while the workplace became more diverse, the sporting landscape became a protected space and male preserve for heterosexual men. Through cultural and legal changes, women have begun to infiltrate these male-only spaces in numbers that reflect more than token individuals. Importantly, despite women becoming normalized in the sporting world, the male preserve has morphed and taken on a more insidious method, whereby women are "allowed" into these spaces and then face constant harassment across numerous areas in the sport industry (Matthews, 2016), and this is particularly true in social media formats. Drew Magary, an accomplished novel writer and blogger for *Deadspin* cum *Defector*, wrote a confessional tale about his progressive development as a male sportswriter while taking care not to absolve his past sins in his article *The Reckoning Always Comes* (2017). The article neatly articulates how the notion of sport as male preserve has morphed over time, and that there is still a large market for the hypermasculine "sport bro" on social media, including popular blog sites and X exchanges. However heinous social media has become towards women, many perpetrators of this harassment are protected by their right to express themselves freely.

Harassment

Numerous academic articles exist that detail the various ways female sport media members have been stalked (Demir and Ayhan, 2022), harassed sexually and otherwise (Garcia & Proffitt, 2022), as well as threatened with violence (Everbach, 2018). In short, females in the sport industry – be they executives, media members, or athletes who are active on social media platforms such as Instagram and X in ways that help legitimize their work and are consistent with their male counterparts' forays into the social media landscape – face constant backlash from other social media users. Some social media sites will lock an abusive user's account, but that does not prevent them from creating a "burner" (a.k.a. an alternative account not directly linked to an identifiable person) and continuing the harassment, inspiring others to continue the harassment for them. The challenge with this is that it is exceedingly difficult to "police" their harassers from a legal standpoint (Kusz & Hodler, 2023).

IOC Consensus Statement

In 2007 the International Olympic Committee (IOC) adopted a Consensus Statement on Sexual Harassment and Abuse in Sport (Leahy, 2008), which was intended to officially recognize and initiate ways to protect athletes from several types of harassment and harm (sexual, abuse, neglect, psychological, and physical). It initially found that "all ages and types of athletes are susceptible to these problems, but science confirms that elite, disabled, child, and lesbian/gay/ bisexual/trans-sexual (LGBT) athletes are at the highest risk" (Mountjoy et al., 2016, p. 1). However, the Consensus Statement pre-dated the proliferation of social media. The 2016 update to this statement acknowledges that social media has provided space for an uptick in and round-the-clock perpetration of harassment for athletes on, in, and through social media platforms.

Case 5.2   Updated IOC Consensus Statement

Cyber harassment and abuse comes in a variety of forms:

1 Grooming of young people with a view towards sexual abuse (online and real world) being perpetrated. This may involve contact from individuals who are not known to the child or young person in their day-to-day life.
2 Sending or receiving sexual messages or images, known as 'sexting'.
3 Use of camera phones to take illicit photographs, including inside sprots facilities (particularly changing rooms) and use of the images for sexual exploitation (sometimes called 'sextortion').
4 Receiving unwanted negative content such as hate messages, exposure to sexual and violent content, and pro-self-harm or pro-eating disorder/body dysmorphia sites.
5 Risks to an individual's reputation from sharing of inappropriate content and/or from creation of false online profiles and impersonation of an individual.
6 Grooming of young people with a view to perpetuate corruption (online and real world) for match fixing and associated activities, which may breach sports' integrity rules and/or constitute criminal offences.
7 Theft of personal and identity data, which may constitute a criminal offense.

Sources: Mountjoy et al., 2016 https://stillmed.olympic.org/media/Document%20Library/OlympicOrg/IOC/What-We-Do/Protecting-Clean-Athletes/Safeguarding/IOC-Consensus-Statement_Harassment-and-abuse-in-sport-2016.pdf

---

It is admirable that the IOC has acknowledged that harassment and harm exist in the world of elite sports, because recognition can be the first step toward mitigation and reconciliation. However, the report admits that the ease with which harassers can communicate with elite athletes via social media has created an issue whereby the pure volume of damaging communication is overwhelming and nearly impossible to police from a legal standpoint. Indeed, the report could only point to a few times where children were protected and a high-profile case when tennis star Serena Williams was able to have a man arrested and detained for stalking and cyber-stalking (Seltzer, 2011), but only after he was physically present in her home.

Case 5.3 New Zealand and Australia Attempt to Address Death Threats via Social Media

In 2021, following a spate of hateful attacks, death wishes, and death threats against athletes in New Zealand sport organizations, that country worked with online safety groups to help support social media managers for clubs and athletes to combat these forms of hateful communication. Fans who attend games and utilize such language can be banned, but athletes note that it is difficult to ignore them on social media. Athletes in New Zealand do have legal options based on the Harmful Digital Communications Act of 2015, "which made it illegal to post harmful messages, damaging images or comments online" (Reid, 2021). The punishment for serious offenses of this nature is up to two years in jail or fines of up to $50,000. However, athletes have been wary to pursue legal action, due, in part, to a mixture of not wanting to relive the trauma, time, and the social and personal costs that come with a lawsuit over cyberbullying.

Meanwhile, in Australia, several sport organizations worked with the government's eSafety Commissioner to help combat online abuse. The Commissioner of eSafety in Australia, Julie Inman Grant, suggests that social media can often be just another source where homophobia, sexism, and racism is perpetuated. Since 2021, she has "overseen significant increases in the eSafety office's budget, increased staffing levels and launched the global Safety by Design initiative" (eSafety Commissioner, 2023). In so doing, Grant has been able to implement regulations such as the Online Safety Act and other reforms to help make social media a more positive space for athletes and sport clubs.

Sources: www.esafety.gov.au/about-us/who-we-are/about-the-commissioner

www.rnz.co.nz/news/sport/455966/athletes-facing-big-challenge-from-online-abuse

---

Sexual Harassment in Esports

Online video game competitions, often referred to as esports, would seem to be a space where women and men can compete on an "even playing field," because the physiological advantages afforded to participants based on sex at the elite levels are seemingly erased. However, the prevalence of sexual harassment in the esporting world would seem to be in evidence. Indeed "due to anonymity, online spaces can facilitate discrimination and hostility toward women and other underrepresented groups . . . almost half (49%) of adolescents who play video games reported experiences with hateful, fascist, or sexist behavior" (Ruvalcaba et al., 2018, p. 298). This typically takes place via social media networks where fans interact with participants and/or communicate about the participants' performances with other fans. Holden et al. (2020) detail some of the difficulty in preventing sexual harassment in esports, but also pose the notion that not addressing this issue could cause legal issues in the future – particularly if esports gamers unionize.

Abuse

In addition to the various forms of harassment that take place via social media, the IOC Consensus Statement details the fact that sexual abuse, maltreatment, and trolling are features of the cyberworld. Children and underrepresented groups are often viewed most at-risk, because this space allows for predators to act in relative anonymity. They can groom and abuse from afar without ever coming in contact with the victim until it is too late to stop the mistreatment. Again, these issues are much more difficult to combat from a legal standpoint than the already challenging ways this is conducted in the "real world." Sanderson and Weathers (2020, pp. 245–7) point out that sport is uniquely situated as an ideal site of abuse for children by detailing five reasons why:

1. Sport is perceived to be a sacred culture, which means that it can be viewed as a space separate from "real-world concerns."
2. Child athletes spend significant time, often in intimate quarters, with peers and coaches.
3. Cultural norms within sport means that abuse is "normalized."
4. Sport organizations have unclear reporting mechanisms for abuse.
5. Power imbalances exist between adults and children in the sporting context.

Snapchat and Child Sexual Abuse in Sport

Though there are instances of strangers engaging in using social media to engage in grooming and child sexual abuse, it is more often the case that the victim knows their assailant (Sanderson & Weathers, 2020). With regard to child sexual abuse (CSA) and social media, it is typically coaches who have been found to be using web applications to create the context from which they can abuse children (Sanderson & Weathers, 2020). One of the most effective means of doing so has been Snapchat, because the content disappears over time, meaning that unless the victim takes screenshots of communication, the grooming and abuse can be lost in the ether.

Sanderson and Weathers (2020) conducted a study on CSA on Snapchat in a sporting context and found nearly 100 examples of it. According to the study, most of the cases held a similar pattern with slightly different details and motivations. Generally, there was a power imbalance between coach and child-athlete, and Snapchat was a tool used to groom and set up a situation where the child-athlete can feel "safe" in posting sexual content because it disappears, and then the coach continued this pattern until they were caught. Since there were children involved, there appeared to be more actual punitive outcomes for alleged perpetrators than in cases involving adults (Sanderson & Weathers, 2020).

Maltreatment

Social media is more than just an opportunity for CSA, and some studies have found that athletes can experience various forms of abuse on a variety of platforms. Kavanah et al. (2016, p. 787) created a rudimentary typology of virtual maltreatment to help readers visualize and categorize what this may look like. Essentially, it is broken down into direct (social media communication from one person to another) and non-direct communication (social media communication about someone) that can be viewed as physically, sexually, or psychologically harmful and often includes forms of discrimination centered on gender, racial, sexual, religious, and disability differences. Non-direct discriminatory forms of maltreatment will be explored in further length in chapter 6 of this manuscript, because again those types of harm are difficult for athletes to place in a legal realm.

Physical

Physical maltreatment is usually centered on threats of violence from one person to another or to degrade, in some way, an individual's physical appearance. Emma Jane (2014a, 2014b) refers to this as one form of "e-bile," whereby users feel safe to freely attack an individual and threaten to injure or worse another person. In the emotionally charged world of sport, this abuse can often take place after poor performances on the field and/or victories by unpopular athletes. Kavanah et al. (2020) detail how athletes Wayne Rooney (Premier League soccer), Beth Tweddle (Olympic gymnast), Andy Murray (tennis), Mark Sanchez (NFL), Serena Williams (tennis), and Maron Bartoli (tennis) were all physically threatened in post-match or -game settings.

Sexual

Sexual maltreatment often include threats of rape or sexual assault. Jane (2014a, 2014b) painstakingly and painfully details numerous examples of how high-profile female athletes, members of the media, and others associated with sport are victims of direct threats of sexual violence that "the anonymous or quasi-anonymous status of the perpetrators – along with the congenerous qualities and prevalence of their communications – also has the effect of erasing the individual and coalescing all these mephitic voices into one" (p. 566). This is also where social media sites such as *Barstool Sports* comes into play, with their seeming celebration that sports are a playground for "boys being boys," which includes the degrading sexual treatment of other women and men (Kusz & Hodler, 2023).

Case 5.4   French Soccer Sex Tape Lawsuit

Karim Benzema is a legendary French soccer player who is a key performer for the international side and striker for Real Madrid who won the Ballon d'Or for best men's soccer player of the calendar year in 2022. In 2015, his teammate Mathieu Valbuena was blackmailed after having a recording of Benzema engaging in sexual relations on a mobile phone. Authorities alleged that Benzema was a part of the group of individuals who attempted to coerce Valbuena (Willsher, 2015). Though Benzema maintained his innocence, there was overwhelming evidence that he had taken part in the scheme, and he was banned from the French National team for six years (Wanjiku, 2022). Benzema was also found guilty of participating in the scheme and received a one-year suspended sentence and fine of $87,000 USD.

Case 5.5   Successful Social Media Lawsuit in the United States

Terry Bollea, better known as the WWF/WCW/WWE superstar Hulk Hogan, was recorded having sex with his best friend's wife in 2006. In 2012, Gawker media, which was the parent media company of seven blogs, published a two-minute edited clip of the interaction on one of its websites. Hogan sued for "infringement of rights of publicity, invasion of privacy, and intentional infliction of emotional distress" (Litigation Finance Journal, 2022). Gawker had been unsuccessfully sued previously over the publication of sexually explicit content that often revealed that sport and sport media celebrities were behaving in misogynist ways (namely Brett Favre, an NFL quarterback, and Sean Salisbury, a former NFL quarterback working at ESPN).

However, this time Bollea was backed financially by billionaire Peter Thiel, who had been outed as homosexual by Gawker media in

2007. He attempted to sue for libel, but since it was true, Gawker was protected. Thiel harbored a grudge and used Bollea's case as a means to gain retribution against Gawker, and the case hinged on the sex tape not being considered newsworthy. In 2016 Bollea prevailed and was awarded $140 million by a jury and later settled for $31 million. This effectively bankrupted Gawker and created a blueprint for the wealthy to protect themselves, deservedly or not, against social media outlets.

Case 5.6 Social Media Abuse of Maxime Comtois in Canada

In a 2019 World Junior Ice Hockey Championship quarterfinal matchup between Canada and Finland, 19-year-old Maxime Comtois, the Canadian captain who was playing through a separated shoulder, was tasked with taking a penalty shot in overtime with a chance to send his team to the semifinals. Comtois was stonewalled at the net, and four minutes later Finland scored a goal to eliminate Team Canada. After the loss, Comtois was subject to a barrage of abuse through a variety of social media sites that were characterized as "anti-francophone racism" (Vomiero, 2019), and it became so pervasive that he shut down the ability for others to comment on his social media platforms for a period of time.

The difficulty with policing social media abuse became apparent as Hockey Canada was left with little ability to pursue legal recourse against those posting hurtful comments toward Comtois. They cited the EPL group Kick It Out, who suggested that there were about 17,000 abusive messages posted towards soccer players during the 2014–2015 season. For his part, Comtois has chosen to use his platform as an NHL player for the Anaheim Ducks to continue to speak out against online social media abuse toward athletes.

Source: https://globalnews.ca/news/4816850/social-media-hate-maxime-comtois-onilne-abuse/

Emotional

Emotional maltreatment usually happens in the wake of a poor performance on the field of play and can include "rumor spreading, ridiculing, terrorizing, humiliating, isolating, belittling, and scapegoating" (Kavanagh et al., 2016, p. 790). This form of behavior is often expressed in ways that poke fun at deeply personal issues an athlete has had to overcome and/or contend with.

Future of Legal Issues in Social Media and Sport

Throughout this chapter, the way the legal landscape looks around social media and sport makes it seem like a cesspool of social, emotional, and sexual violence – a veritable free-for-all whereby just about anyone can say anything without recourse, no matter who it hurts or how they hurt them. And for the most part it is. Right now, there are very few instances where victims of cyberbullying, harassment, and/or abuse have been sided with in the court system. Further, in those instances, it either requires physical evidence of harm being conducted beyond social media statements or the financing of a billionaire and his lawyer.

This leads us to ask two questions by way of conclusion:

1 What can we learn from the patterns of behavior around legal issues that have taken place over social media?
2 How can this be tempered or combatted?

As of now, the best policy may be to stay away from controversial issues and things that may cause distress for the user, but that seems silly to do in the social media era. Further, this book is about social media and sport, so what good would that do? Rather, and as other academics, the IOC, and multiple institutions have suggested, perhaps there is room for a definition of what constitutes hate speech and how to police it on a variety of sites that would make the social-mediascape a safer, more welcoming, and legally covered site for information sharing.

References

Adler, D., & Kelly, M. (2022). Pitchers who have thrived in elimination games. *MLB. com*. www.mlb.com/news/best-clutch-pitchers-in-mlb-history-c298312438

Baccarella, C., Wagner, T., Kietzmann, J., & McCarthy, I. (2018). Social media? It's serious! Understanding the dark side of social media. *European Management Journal, 36*(4), 431–438.

Bill of Rights Institute. (2023). Constitution of the United States, 1–15. Retrieved April 20, 2023 from https://bri-docs.s3.amazonaws.com/Branded-Constitution.pdf

Bustad, J., & Mower, R. (2018). Welcome to the factory. In R. King-White (ed.) *Sport and the neoliberal university: Profit, politics and pedagogy* (pp. 193–207). New Brunskwick, NJ: Rutgers University Press.

Epstein, A., & Anderson, P. (2015). The Relationship between a collegiate student-athlete and the university: An Historical and legal perspective. *Marquette Sports Law Review, 26*(2), 287–300.

eSafetyCommissioner (2023). *About the Commissioner*. Australian Government. www. esafety.gov.au/about-us/who-we-are/about-the-commissioner

Demir, Y., & Ayhan, B. (2022). Being a female sports journalist on Twitter: Online harassment, sexualization and hegemony. *International Journal of Sport Communication, 15*(3), 207–217.

Draper, K. (2016). ESPN fires Curt Schilling, who finally became too much of an embarrassment. *Deadspin*. Accessed April 20, 2023 from https://deadspin.com/espn-fires-curt-schilling-who-finally-became-too-much-1772165466

Draper, K., & Belson, K. (2017). Jemele Hill suspended by ESPN after response to Jerry Jones. *The New York Times*. Accessed April 20, 2023 from https://www.nytimes.com/2017/10/09/sports/football/jemele-hill-suspended-espn.html

Dunning, E. (1986). Sport as a male preserve: Notes on the social sources of masculine identity and its transformations. *Theory, Culture & Society*, *3*(1), 79–90.

Everbach, T. (2018). "I realized it was about them…not me": Women sports journalists and harassment. In J. Vickery and T. Everbach (eds.) *Mediating misogyny: Gender, technology, and harassmen* (pp. 131–149). Cham, Switzerland: Palgrave Macmillon.

Forde, P., & Dellenger, R. (2023). NCAA issues first NIL ruling, with Cavinder twins at the center of it. *Sports Illustrated*. Accessed April 20, 2023 from https://www.si.com/college/2023/02/24/cavinder-twins-miami-womens-basketball-infractions-nil-ncaa

Garcia, C., & Proffitt, J. (2022). Recontextualizing barstool sports and misogyny in online US sports media. *Communication & Sport*, *10*(4), 730–745.

Harrigan, F. (2020). Free speech restrictions put college athletes at risk. *Deseret News*. Accessed April 20, 2023 from https://www.deseret.com/opinion/2020/12/18/22187719/free-speech-restrictions-college-athletes-social-media-journalists-social-justice-message-punishment

Harvey, D. (1999). Time-space compression and the postmodern condition. In M. Waters (ed.) *Modernity critical concepts* (pp. 98–118). London: Routledge.

Heslam, J. (2008). ESPN suspends columnist Jemele Hill. *Boston Herald*. Accessed April 20, 2023 from https://www.bostonherald.com/2008/06/18/espn-suspends-columnist-jemele-hill/

Hill, J. (2017a, September 13). Donald Trump is a white supremacist who has largely surrounded himself w/ other white supremacists [Tweet]. *Twitter*. https://twitter.com/jemelehill/status/907391978194849793?lang=en

Hill, J. (2017b, September 11). Trump is the most ignorant, offensive president of my lifetime: His rise is a direct result of white supremacy: Period [Tweet]. *Twitter*. https://twitter.com/jemelehill/status/907392882155425793?lang=en

Hill, J. (2017c, September 11). He has surrounded himself with white supremacists – No they are not "alt right" – And you want me to believe he isn't a white supremacist? [Tweet]. *Twitter*. https://twitter.com/jemelehill/status/907393203762073600

Hill, J. (2017d, September 11). He is unqualified and unfit to be president [Tweet]. *Twitter*. https://twitter.com/jemelehill/status/907393929087262720

Holden, J., Baker III, T., & Edelman, M. (2020). The #E-too movement: Fighting back against sexual harassment in electronic sports. *Arizona State Law Journal*, 1–46.

Holloway, D. (2016). Curt Schilling fires back at ESPN over dismissal. *Variety*. Accessed April 20, 2023 from https://variety.com/2016/tv/news/curt-schilling-espn-fires-back-1201759177/

Jane, E. (2014a). "Your a ugly, whorish, slut" understanding e-bile. *Feminist Media Studies*, *14*(4), 531–546.

Jane, E. (2014b). "Back to the kitchen, cunt": Speaking the unspeakable about online misogyny. *Continuum*, *28*(4), 558–570.

Kavanagh, E., Jones, I., & Sheppard-Marks, L. (2016). Towards typologies of virtual maltreatment: Sport, digital cultures & dark leisure. *Leisure Studies*, *35*(6), 783–796.

King-White, R. (2022). "I didn't ask for any of this": (White) privilege, the American (dream) family, and health care. *Cultural StudiesóCritical Methodologies, 22*(5), 533–543.

King-White, R., & Giardina, M. (2023). Parenting in pandemic times: Notes on the emotional geography of youth sport culture. In. D. Andrews, H. Thorpe & J. Newman (Eds.) *Sport and Physical Culture in Global Pandemic Times: COVID Assemblages* (pp. 445–469). Cham: Springer International Publishing.

Kusz, K., & Hodler, M. (2023). "Saturdays are for the boys": Barstool sports and the cultural politics of white fratriarchy in contemporary America. *Sociology of Sport Journal, 40*(1), 96–107.

Kyodo News. (2021). *Olympic Athletes Pained By Online Bashing, Mental Health Care Sought*. https://english.kyodonews.net/news/2021/07/13be0e90b1a9-olympic-athletes-pained-by-online-bashing-mental-health-care-sought.html

Leahy, T. (2008). Understanding and preventing sexual harassment and abuse in sport: Implications for the sport psychology profession. *International Journal of Sport and Exercise Psychology, 6*(4), 351–353.

Lever, K. (2022). Censorship in college athletics, what you need to know. *2aDays*. Accessed April 20, 2023 from https://www.2adays.com/blog/censorship-in-college-athletics-what-you-need-to-know/

Litigation Finance Journal (2022). *The 5th Anniversary of the Peter Thiel/Hulk Hogan/Gawker Case: What Have We Learned?* https://litigationfinancejournal.com/the-6th-anniversary-of-the-peter-thiel-hulk-hogan-gawker-case-what-have-we-learned/

Magary, D. (2017). The Reckoning always comes. *Deadspin*. Accessed April 20, 2023 from https://deadspin.com/the-reckoning-always-comes-1819874125

Matthews, C. (2016). The Tyranny of the male preserve. *Gender & Society, 30*(2), 312–333.

Mayer, K. (2013). Colleges and universities all atwitter: Constitutional implications of regulating. *Marquette Sports Law Review, 23*(2), 455–477.

Moskovitz, D. (2015). Various lowlights from Curt Schilling's failed 38Studios. *Deadspin*. Accessed April 20, 2023 from https://deadspin.com/various-lowlights-from-curt-schillings-failed-38-studio-1732879364

Mountjoy, M. Brackenridge, C., Arrington, M., Blauwet, C., Carska-Sheppard, A., Fastin, K., Kirby, S., Leahy, T., Marks, S., Martin, K., Starr, K., Tiivas, A., & Budgett, R. (2016). The IOC consensus statement: Harassment and abuse (non-accidental violence) in sport. *British Journal of Sports Medicine*, 1–11.

O'Hallarn, B., Shapiro, S., Hambrick, M., Wittkower, D., Ridinger, L., & Morehead, C. (2018). Sport, Twitter hashtags, and the public sphere: A Qualitative test of the phenomenon through a Curt Schilling case study. *Journal of Sport Management, 32*(4), 389–400.

Paul, K. (2021). Internet freedom on the decline in US and globally, study finds. *The Guardian*. Accessed April 20, 2023 from https://www.theguardian.com/technology/2021/sep/21/internet-freedom-decline-free-speech-study

Reid, F. (2021). Athletes facing big challenge from online abuse. *RNZ*. www.rnz.co.nz/news/sport/455966/athletes-facing-big-challenge-from-online-abuse

Ruane, K. (2014). *Freedom of speech and press: Exceptions to the First Amendement*. Washington, D.C., Congressional Research Service.

Ruvalcaba, O., Shulze, J., Kim, A., Berzenski, S., & Otten, M. (2018). Women's experiences in esports: Gendered differences in peer and spectator feedback during competitive video game play. *Journal of Sport and Social Issues, 42*(4), 295–311.

Sanderson, J., & Weathers, M. (2020). Snapchat and child sexual abuse in sport: Protecting child athletes in the social media age. *Sport Management Review*, *23*(1), 81–94.
Sawyer, T., Bemiller, J., & Trendafilova, S. (2012). Social media and free speech in education and sport. *Journal of Physical Education, Recreation & Dance*, *83*(1), 7–56.
Seltzer, A. (2011). Man arrested for stalking Serena Williams. *The Palm Beach Post*. Accessed April 20, 2023 from https://www.palmbeachpost.com/story/news/crime/2011/05/03/man-arrested-for-stalking-serena/7469214007/
Theberge, N. (1985). Toward a feminist alternative to sport as a male preserve. *Quest*, *37*(2), 193–202.
Umar, T. (2015). Total eclipse of the tweet: How Social media restrictions on student and professional athletes affect free speech. *Jeffrey S. Moorad Sports Law Journal*, *22*(1), 311–351.
Vomiero, J. (2019). Hate against team Canada captain on social media shines light on athlete abuse online: Experts. *Global News*. https://globalnews.ca/news/4816850/social-media-hate-maxime-comtois-onilne-abuse/
Wallance, G. (2017). White House interfered with Jemele Hill's right of free expression. *The Hill*. Accessed April 20, 2023 from https://thehill.com/opinion/whitehouse/350729-the-trump-administration-interfered-with-jemele-hills-right-of-free/
Wanjiku, B. (2022). The Karim Benzema story: From being banned from the France national team to winning the Ballon d'Or. *Sports Brief*. Accessed April 20, 2023 from https://sportsbrief.com/football/26452-the-karim-benzema-story-banned-france-national-team-winning-ballon-dor/
West, S. (2018). Suing the President for first amendment violations. *Oklahoma Law Review*, *71*(1), 321–346.
Willsher, K. (2015). Karim Benzema to remain in police custody over sex-tape blackmail case. *The Guardian*. Accessed April 20, 2023 from https://www.theguardian.com/football/2015/nov/04/karim-benzema-arrested-sex-tape-blackmail
Yeung, J., Jozuka, E., & Benoza, K. (2022). Japan makes "online insults" punishable by one year in prison in wake of reality tv star's death. *CNN*. www.cnn.com/2022/06/14/asia/japan-cyberbullying-law-intl-hnk-scli/index.html

6 Social Media and Social Issues

Social media, as a site of cultural communication, has radically transformed everyday life. No longer are (sport) media consumers forced to read reports from the fairly monochromatic, and often dogmatic, interpretive lens provided by the overwhelmingly white men who worked as journalists in the newsroom or talking heads on television. For those minorities who became the some of the first non-white, male, or heterosexual members of the media, the response from readers and/or viewers was almost always negative. Howard Bryant (a noted black sports journalist who has written several books, numerous newspapers, ESPN, and more recently Meadowlark Media) recently suggested that he began to keep a "go back to Africa file" (Braude, 2020) during his early days as a sport journalist in order to cope with the treatment. The backlash most certainly remains, but the (minority) voices have multiplied.

Throughout this book, we have alluded to the notion that this relatively new development has helped provide space for the sharing of alternative viewpoints that can help people reach new levels of understanding about the conditions and contexts from which others experience everyday life. It is also possible, however, to cultivate social media communication feeds that only face inward, that reflect voices that speak to our individual worldviews. To that end, Will Leitch (2015) once wrote:

> We all do this. We all carefully curate our feeds, or our cable channels, or our reading material. We know if we are diligent about it, we can comfortably avoid having to read anything we disagree with. (Safe spaces are only literal on college campuses; the rest of us create them wherever we can.) . . . Voices outside the bubble are suspect, even if they're right. Especially if they're right."
>
> (para. 15)

Social media does not have to be this way.

In this chapter, we will outline the various pathways social media has served to provide the space for new and different voices to communicate with broader audiences. To do so, the chapter breaks down how social media works to open up ways to undermine and (sometimes simultaneously) reify social class, racial, gender/sexuality, and national/global divisions. Throughout we will provide select examples of how this has worked in and through social media via owners/administrators, media members, athletes, and users. By way of conclusion to the book, this chapter will critically reflect on the democratic possibilities that social media has and could provide in such a way that moves beyond "traditions which seek to merely reinforce and reproduce current conditions, a critical and progressive orientation (that) aspires to transform the present and produce a different, better future" (Sage, 1993, p. 161).

Social Media and Social Class

Critical research on the complex relationship between social media and sports has certainly grown over the past few years in academia. There are numerous articles, books, and other forms of communication that quite directly deal with the variety of -isms many people have to contend with in everyday life and in and through the increased connectivity and ability to share thoughts, feelings, images, and videos through the Internet (Filo et al., 2015). However, one area of sociological critique that has been relatively ignored in academia is the relationship between social class and social media. This is unfortunate, but also unsurprising.

Understanding Social Class

First and foremost, social class is a difficult thing to measure and characterize, even though we *know* and *feel* its presence and effects on our everyday lives. French cultural theorist Pierre Bourdieu (1984, 1997) has conducted the most resonant research on the topic and has broken down the ways he understands social class works as threefold:

1 *Economic Capital* – Money and wealth plus the leisure time to be able to enjoy what this can provide. Time is important because without it the resources to experience social class privilege are left wanting.
2 *Social Capital* – The network of people one is around physically and virtually, and the ability to utilize those connections in order to gain access and opportunity where one may not have existed prior. In the world of sports, this could be knowing someone whose business has a suite at a Premier League ballpark or stadium and/or provides more expensive equipment than an individual would be willing to purchase themselves.
3 *Cultural Capital* – The behaviors, language, and taste in dress, music, cars, and food (among other things) that reflect norms in particular groups. This can be experienced in things as small as the type of beverage one selects at a game, places one stays when one travels, and how one gets there.

Social Class and Social Media

In the world of social media, it might seem like social class is erased, because all anyone needs to participate is a device with Internet connectivity. However, this is not the case. Research suggests that there is actually quite a bit of disparity in social media users along the social class continuum. Data indicates that individuals on the higher end of the social class scale tend to use at least three social media platforms when compared to just one in the lower class, and the types of social media sites people use vary along class lines as well. "Notably, Twitter is more likely to be used by professionals, in comparison with other groups. Facebook and Myspace have a more even spread in use across the class groups, but still with an overrepresentation of higher professional class groups" (Yates & Lockley, 2018, p. 1305). What does this mean and how does it get expressed in the world of sports?

Social Class, Social Media, and Sport

Put simply, even as social media has leveled the communications playing field, in that more people have the ability to share views, ideas, and their everyday lives, social media platforms still privilege those with means. Case in point, in 2014, Daniel Snyder, owner of the Washington Redskins (now renamed The Commanders)[1] of the NFL, was facing heavy criticism for the team's racist nickname (Sharrow et al., 2021). In response, he hired the public relations firm Burson-Marsteller to create a fictional grassroots team support group called "Redskins Facts" replete with a website and X account that propped up weakly conducted "research studies," false historical narratives, and garnered the support of a number of former players to fight the movement against the team nickname (Levin & Stahl, 2014). Though this attempt was later discovered by popular media such as *Slate* and *The Daily Show* (Stewart, 2014), Redskins Facts was able to reach numerous people with their dubious "facts" via *Sports Illustrated*, *The Washington Post*, and X by paying for ad space at each source. This was even more insidious on X where, at first glance, Redskins Facts looked and read like a post written by someone that a user followed.

Though this ridiculous act was discovered and shamed (Petchesky, 2014), it speaks to the power and ability those from the upper class have to communicate with and reach more people by simply paying for it. Even a cursory glance at who, in the sports world, have (and now pay for) verified checkmarks on X, become influencers on YouTube, and so on, followed by basic research as to where they come from in terms of wealth and/or family background, reveals that it is usually someone from the upper or upper-middle class in terms of access to (or a combination of) social, cultural, or economic capital (Yates & Lockley, 2018). In other words, even in the world of social media, "class matters" (Ehrenreich, 2021). What this means is that each of the topics to follow must also be linked back to its relationship with social class. Those that have the ability to communicate with more people and, often, more effectively often have access to, as well as utilize and wield, their various forms of capital in ways to be heard, read, and experienced more than an "everyday" user of social media.

Case 6.1 LIV Golf and Social Media

In June 2022 professional golf legend, Greg Norman, teamed with Saudi Arabian funders and current PGA athletes Phil Mickelson, Brooks Koepka, and Patrick Reid to create a competitor to the PGA – LIV Golf. The controversial decision rankled many in the golf industry and golf fans, who tend to hold upper-class and conservative viewpoints (Millard, 2023). The well-funded outfit was created in an effort to help "sportswash" global views about Saudi Arabia, which has a horrible human rights record, while also providing professional golfers with stability and financial security heretofore not realized within the PGA (Boykoff, 2022).

Despite the strong backing from Saudi Arabia, LIV struggled to gain a television partner to cover their events and was initially only ever aired over YouTube's streaming platform (Hamel, 2023). Some LIV golfers including Greg Norman, Talor Gooch, and Cameron Smith experienced great growth in their social media following, whereas others including Phil Mickelson, Bubba Watson, and Lee Westwood lost thousands (Carpenter, 2023). Players who defected from the PGA to LIV cited the massive and guaranteed paydays, reduced playing schedule, and increased free time to be with family as reasons for making the switch.

Recently, the PGA and LIV announced a merger that "stands to reshape golf's economic structure profoundly, bringing the business ventures of the PGA Tour, LIV Golf and the DP World Tour, formerly the European Tour, into a new company" (Blinder et al., 2023). Despite the mixed reaction to and low ratings for LIV Golf on social media, the entity promises to reshape working conditions for professional golfers who, to date, generally live fairly nomadic and precarious laboring lives (save for a few top earners such as Tiger Woods, Rory McIlroy, and Mickelson). Given the fiscal support for this new (as yet unnamed) golf enterprise, it may well serve to diversify the professional golfing ranks when all is said and done.

Sources: www.nytimes.com/2023/06/27/sports/golf/pga-tour-liv-golf-merger-obstacles.html

www.expressvpn.com/stream-sports/golf/liv-golf/?msclkid=3aced6c46c1f11ce976bb25802c51f7a

https://golfweek.usatoday.com/2023/05/26/liv-golf-news-tournament-broadcast-youtube-pay-per-view/

Social Media and Race

Understanding Race

Carl Linnaeus is often acknowledged as the first scientist who classified human beings into four distinct races: Europeans (whitish), Americans (reddish), Asians (tawny), and Africans (blackish) (Muller-Wille, 2014). His work, completed in 1735, served to inform most research on race in the years to follow (Jackson, Rubin & Weidman, 2005) and was utilized in myriad dangerous ways. For example, it allowed for the United States, a country founded on the belief that "all men are created equal," to justify slavery, and later served as a means for the legal segregation, mistreatment, and sometimes "ethnic cleansing" of others in places such as South Africa, Germany, Australia, and Bosnia and Herzegovina during the 20th century. Though fissures in the logic and findings of these studies began to show, it was not until the Human Genome Project's 13-year journey that there was strong scientific evidence counter to this work. The HGP began in 1990 and was completed in 2003, generating the first human genome sequencing where scientists were able to pull apart, decode, and understand "the human blueprint".

> In 2003, Phase 1 of the Human Genome Project (HGP) demonstrated that humans populating the earth today are on average 99.99% identical at the DNA level, there is no genetic basis for race, and there is more genetic variation within a race than between them ... thus, the idea of 'race' as a genetic category was presumably put to rest.
> (Duello et al., 2021, p. 232)

With regard to connecting race to health and social class, Nancy Krieger (2000) found:

1. That "race" is a social construct, forged through oppression, slavery, and conquest, whereby self-defined racially dominant groups benefit economically, socially, and politically from their legally and/or social sanctioned exploitation and oppression of those they brand as racially inferior;
2. That racial/ethnic inequalities in health reflect, in part, racial/ethnic socioeconomic disparities in work, wealth, income education, housing, and overall standard of living; and
3. That racial/ethnic inequalities in health are nonetheless not reducible to class inequalities in health, given experiences of racial discrimination within and across socioeconomic strata.

(p. 211)

At the time, the HGP's findings around race were stunning to a world that had spent 300 years thinking of "race as science." However, the power of the social, cultural, and historical vestiges of racial "science" remains over a generation post-HGP. Race is not real, but it is "real" in the sense that it is a lived reality for nearly every human being on planet Earth.

Race and Sport: A (Very) Brief History

Given the fact that sports provide a space for physical, mental, and emotional superiority to play out in an arena, ballfield, or pitch, it can be a site where pseudo-scientific beliefs linking race to on- and off-field achievements, failures, and essential characteristics about race get reified. Historically, it was assumed that white athletes had the biological makeup to be superior in almost any athletic endeavor – outside of black jockeys at the horse track (Leeds & Rockoff, 2019). In the early 1900s, Jack Johnson began to shatter that belief by besting numerous white opponents in the boxing ring while upsetting white people and middle-class blacks by having sex with white women (Alderman et al., 2018). Later, during World War II, Jesse Owens defeated Hitler's supposed top athletes on the track while Joe Louis defeated Max Schmelling as millions gathered around the radio to listen to the first black athletes to capture the heart of Americans (McReae, 2014).

After blacks and other minorities were allowed on the baseball and football fields and on the basketball court, the myth of the superior white athlete was usurped by the "naturally" athletic black athlete able to dominate in these sports and further feed the mythmaking. More to the point, while it is true that black athletes are overrepresented in these professional sports relative to their numbers in the population, it would be more accurate to link this domination back to social class distinctions because these are sports where access to higher education, money, and upward social mobility became possible in the United States. Globally, in sports, where one can most cheaply enter and possibly experience upward social mobility (think soccer, baseball, and basketball), these patterns of (social class and racial) minority overrepresentation are apparent. Conversely, in sports most closely tied to amateurism, wealth, and exclusivity such as fencing, equestrian, and rowing/crew this works in reverse, and a majority of college, high school, and youth sports are dominated by those with access to more capital (read: white and upper-middle class) (Azzarito & Harrison, Jr., 2008). Yet the notion of the naturally superior, deviant, and untrustworthy minority athlete persists, and in the social media realm, the mythmaking and racism have become extreme.

> **Case 6.2 Racism and German Soccer**
>
> The vestiges of racism that partially fueled World War II remain in Germany nearly a century after the conflict. In 2021 the German Center for Integration and Migration Research (DeZIM) produced an analysis of media coverage, academic papers, and legal documents in addition to nearly 5,000 telephone interviews about racism in the country (Furstenau, 2022). The project found that nearly 25% of Germans had been negatively affected by racism during their lives, and 90% suggest that they live in a "racist society."
>
> It should be no surprise that social media provides space for racist abuse, language, and behaviors. Indeed, during the U17 and U21 European championships in 2023, racial minorities on both teams reported that they were subjected to "a strong accumulation of racist comments" (Associated Press, 2023). On the U21 side, Youssoufa Moukoko and Jessic Ngankam, both Black, stated that negative racially charged comments and monkey emojis were posted to their social media accounts following a 1–1 draw with Israel in which both players missed penalty kicks. Moukoko lamented this reaction, suggesting "if we win we are all Germans. If we lose, then these monkey comments arrive. Jessic received them, I've received them. Things like this simply do not belong in football" (AP, 2023). The U17 team endured similar abuse but chose to ignore the posts, even citing it as a catalyst for bringing the team closer as they went on to win the entire tournament.
>
> Sources: https://apnews.com/article/germany-u17-soccer-racism-1d1259c6956ab6b669424ccce8c70e8f
>
> www.dw.com/en/racism-in-germany-is-part-of-everyday-life/a-61700339
>
> https://apnews.com/article/germany-racism-european-u21-championship-a5540152e1a64f8ce306f49acb97fdc4

Racism and Social Media

Indeed Farrington et al. (2015) suggest that since race, as genetic or biological fact, has been undone by the HGP, the impulse by many who have historically benefitted from the hierarchical privileges afforded by racist science is to double down. They point out that yes there have been numerous efforts in the United Kingdom and other countries to "stamp out racism" from an organizational level, but that there is almost no controlling fans, media members, employees, and players desire to hang on to the past. "In short, social media is providing an outlet for the mass publication and sharing of racist views and abuse" (2015, p. 3). Sports organization message boards, X, Facebook, Instagram, podcasts, and blogs have provided the platform for content creators, podcast producers, users, readers, and listeners to posit racist diatribes on a variety of subjects (e.g., Baker & Rowe, 2013; Cleland, 2014; Hylton & Lawrence, 2016; Love et al., 2019; Oshiro et al., 2021).

Anti-Racism and Social Media

Social media surely presents a challenge in combatting racists and racism in that anyone can present unscientific beliefs that others can take on as "truths," and there is no stopping this from happening. Social media responses to the racist killings of Eric Garner and Trayvon Martin in America would follow an eerily similar pattern. First, they would be met with critical social media posts by athletes such as LeBron James, who donned an "I can't breathe" T-shirt and a hooded sweatshirt in solidarity with both, or the racism of former Los Angeles Clippers owner Donald Sterling, leading to a protest by his players in a playoff game (Hylton & Lawrence, 2016), or Milwaukee Bucks players refusing to play after the racist killing of Jacob Blake that would initially be celebrated by fans of the game and anti-racists alike. Second, racists would provide counter-narratives on social media lambasting these athletes and their supporters as "social justice warriors" (as if that is a bad thing), "reverse racists," or even claim that the former group was too sensitive and "made things about race too much." Third, the two groups would argue, believe their own "truths," and things would simmer until the next unfortunate killing of an innocent minority by agents of the state.

There have been numerous studies utilizing social media to study marginalized sub-cultures – to shed light on inequity in order to promote positive social change in whatever way(s) possible (King-White, 2013). Studies in this vein detail and sometimes critically assess the ways social media has been used to promote or combat things like racism (Kilvington & Price, 2019), but do not do so to great effect. As with all different forms of inequity, race and racism can be and are critically discussed on a variety of social media platforms from popular blogs like *Edge of Sports*, *Defector*, and various substacks, to podcasts such as *The End of Sports*, *Burn it All Down*, and the entire *Meadowlark* catalog, to everyday users who wish for a better tomorrow for everyone. However, similar to the racist tragedies discussed earlier, they are met with racist social media entities who challenge these arguments and/or users who refuse to connect the dots between the racialized modern sociopolitical context and the everyday ways racism is promoted and experienced via social media.

Social Media and Gender/Sexuality

Understanding Sex, Gender, and Sexuality

There has been a blurring of the lines when it comes to modern conceptualizations of and social reactions to the ways people identify and perform their sex, gender, and sexuality. Traditionally, sex differences placed men in a legally, occupationally, economically, and politically hierarchical position of power over women. The second paragraph of the U.S. Declaration of Independence, for instance, reads "all men are created equal" despite the fact that the men writing those words owned slaves, and, importantly for this section, completely excluded women (Maier, 1999). What this means is that in the United States and in most other countries around the world, women's viewpoints, accomplishments, and abilities have always been subjugated and considered *less than* their male counterparts. Thus, this hierarchy has historically privileged men and masculinity in such a way that most societies are considered to be *patriarchal*, and challenges to these norms are often criticized, brushed aside, and/or brutally attacked.

Fissures in this power structure started to show in first-wave feminism as women in the late 1800s to early 1900s worked to gain voting rights and opportunities to work (Rampton, 2019). Their (minor) victories began to show in the voting booths and workplace and were magnified during World War II as countries needed to remain economically viable while men were off fighting. During this time, sex-change operations, namely that of Christine Jorgensen, a former G.I. who underwent hormonal therapy in addition to physical surgery (Meyerowitz, 2004), opened up new conceptualizations of biological versus social sex identification, and alternative sexualities became ever so slightly more accepted (Foucault, 1990). Second, third, and fourth-wave feminism have served to challenge the patriarchal hierarchy in economic, legal, social, and cultural ways (Rampton, 2015) – albeit imperfectly and incompletely, and not without major moments of resistance.

All told, it is probably easiest at this moment to utilize Meyerowitz's (2004, p. 3) tripartite conceptualization of sex, gender, and sexuality to organize this section:

1 *Sex* – Chromosomes, genes, genitals, hormones, and other physical markers, some of which could be modified and some of which could not.
2 *Gender* – Represented masculinity, femininity, and the behaviors commonly associated with them.
3 *Sexuality* – Connoted the erotic, now sorted into a range of urges, fantasies, and behaviors.

She further posits that sex, gender, and sexuality are "constructed categories constantly defined and redefined in social, cultural, and intellectual processes and performances" (p. 3).

The fluidity of sex, gender, and sexualities in society has been complicated by the fact that women are establishing an uneasy foothold in the labor market. Some have conceptualized this as the feminization of the workforce, whereby women are having children later, occupying more positions of power, and making more money than ever before, even if it is still not equal to their male counterparts (King-White, 2022). However, when COVID-19 spread across the globe, women retreated to more traditional work-from-home and nurturing positions (King-White & Giardina, 2023). Sport, too, has been an excellent site to bear witness to the changes in society around sex, gender, and sexuality.

Women in Sport

Historically women have been denied entry into competitive sports or forced to participate in ways that would prevent overexertion, sweating, and linking back to social class, often only those sports that were accessible to those coming from wealthy backgrounds. Tennis was played with whalebone corsets, bicycles were ridden "side-saddle," while swimming, croquet, and figure skating were allowed as long as the latter did not include jumping (Adams, 2011). Everything from underwear (Phillips & Phillips, 1993) to rules (Staurowsky, 2016) to social and cultural conventions have been utilized to delay the advancement of women's sport participation, spectating, and celebration of achievement.

Mirroring, reflecting, and reinforcing the feminization of the workforce and the socio-political advancements by first-wave feminists, women were able to participate in international competitions such as the Olympics albeit under modified rules, and got their first taste of organized professional sport through the All-American Girls Professional Baseball League (Weiller & Higgs, 1994). Yet, as accurately depicted by the film *A League of Their Own*, these women had to play in revealing outfits and go to comportment classes to "prove their femininity" (read: not lesbian) on and off the field in ways that their male counterparts never did (Joan Hult, personal communication).

As the 20th century wore on, second, third, and fourth-wave feminism helped score more victories for women's sports on and off the field. Today women's teams in college basketball have games that are more watched than NBA matchups (Weiner, 2023); the women's U.S. soccer team is more successful and supported in higher numbers than the men's team; alternative sexualities and gendered performances are more accepted; and women like Mina Kimes, Sarah Spain, and Katie Nolan among many others have prominent roles at ESPN and other sport media entities. Things have certainly improved markedly for women in the sports world from the days of six-on-six basketball where defenders could not cross mid-court to today, but there are still massive pay gaps, differential treatment, and suggestions that the women's game is not as fun to watch as the male equivalent persist.

Sexism, Homophobia, and Social Media

One of the more challenging hurdles women have had to deal with in the social media era is the constant drone of having to prove their ability, knowledge, and worth to male consumers, who see their inclusion in the male preserve as an open challenge to previously "male-dominated spaces." Female athletes and media members often must endure catcalls, hate speech, and suggestions that they "go back to the kitchen," and otherwise deal with "e-bile" (Jane, 2014) that pose threats of (sexual) violence on their person via social media sources. Social media sites *Kissing Suzy Kolber*, *Barstool*, early versions of *Deadspin*, and more get hits that lead to more ad revenue by posting sexualized photos and videos of women in scantily clad clothes or in suggestive positions. Social media sites Instagram, Facebook reels, and more inundate users with suggestions that they engage with this content.

Furthermore, those from the LGBTQ+ community who seek to transgress the norms are encountered with even more outrageous reactions from consumers, fans, and competitors. When male athletes like Jason Collins of the NBA, Brittney Griner of the WNBA, or Michael Sam of the NFL came out as homosexual, they were met with fierce backlash as well as welcome and support from social media sources (Cassidy, 2017; Dann & Everbach, 2016; De Ridder & Van Bauwel, 2015). In a similar vein to the ways social media discusses race, sex, gender, and sexuality are often argued over and about with little in the way of actual progressive movement from those discussions. A good example of this was when Lia Thomas, a transgender female, won an NCAA championship in swimming, but was faced with massive backlash on social media sites that called for her being banned and/or her championship to not be recognized (Fraser, 2022).

Case 6.3 Social Media and Sexuality in the Western World

Recent research by Keith Parry and Magrath (2022) suggests that attitudes towards non-heterosexual athletes in the Western world have improved considerably since the new millennia, and numerous LGBTQ+ athletes have been able to garner support from fans and fellow competitors despite and/or because of their identity within the LGBTQ+ community. This is not to suggest that all non-heterosexual athletes are able to participate in sports with full support from teammates, opponents, and fans, or that athletics automatically provides a "safe space" for LGBTQ+ participants, but simply that conditions are better than they were during the height of the AIDS epidemic.

During the COVID pandemic, many fans, fan communities, and athletes turned to social media as a means of connecting with one another. In the UK, this led to the development of online fan networks like the Gay Gooners, who "emerged in 2013" and now "over half of the 92 elite league clubs in English football now have an officially sanction LGBT group, and numerous others in Scotland, too" (Parry & Magrath, 2022). Other countries like Australia and the United States have seen a rise in LGBTQ+ fan bases in online forums. Further, several athletes in the community, such as Brittney Griner, have utilized social media as a platform to bring visibility to their "otherness" – be it sexual or otherwise. Social media can be a source for promoting social acceptance of people who identify with/as alternative sexualities, but given the fact that it is difficult to punish hate speech and cyberbullying, it can also be a source for homophobic slurs and threats towards those who identify as LGBTQ+.

Source: www.emerald.com/insight/content/doi/10.1108/S1476-285420220000015016/full/html

Social Media as Safe Space for Women and LGBTQ+

Social media can also be viewed as a site where women and people who are LGBTQ+ can develop fellowship and community in ways that have heretofore seemed impossible. Without having to physically meet and be "out," digital space can harbor and protect those from marginalized backgrounds. Sites like *The Trevor Project* seek to address the lowered rates of participation in sports and physical activity by transgender and nonbinary athletes regardless of "outness" by providing research, advocacy, support, and community. #LGTBQRIGHTS has become a social media catch-all for the international movement toward the promotion of equal rights and opportunities for all in modern times. Social media has also been a space for suicide prevention, support, and allyship in this realm in ways that make it safer and easier for cisgender allies to lend a helping and supportive hand (Lucas & Hodler, 2018).

Similarly, women in sport have enjoyed some of the benefits and possibilities social media has to offer. For instance, given the consuming public's waning attention span, social media clips of amazing plays, championships won, and emotional moments can be shared on social media that are easily picked up and viewed rather than waiting for "old media" to turn their misogynistic head to focus on women's sports (Vann, 2014). Social media also makes it possible to provide hard evidence to old media and sexists that significant interest in women's sport can and does exist when provided coverage, focus, and attention similar to that of male equivalents (Antunovic & Linden, 2015).

As noted previously, ratings for women's NCAA basketball tournament games are way up and provide a small window into the unique growth opportunity that exists in women's sport that may not be true for men. Case in point is when the Name Image and Likeness (NIL) revision by the NCAA went into effect in July 2021, there was an assumption that male athletes were going to benefit while females would be left behind. What has happened is quite interesting, and does not exactly match up with the assumption. American football and men's basketball players have earned a lot of NIL money, but female athletes who have developed social media and (self-) promotional skills have benefited quite a bit through their deftness in social media. By late 2022, 6 of the top 10 college sports for NIL were women's and have been able to generate more attention for their on-field, on-court, or on-pitch sporting performances that have been ignored in the past (Bilas, 2022). It is clear then that social media can be a platform for dangerous and regressive patriarchal performances and *also* a space of great opportunities for women and the LGBTQ+ community.

Social Media and Nationalism/Globalization

It has been argued cogently that social media has contributed mightily to time-space compression (Harvey, 1999) in a rapidly globalized world. Chapter 4 provides much more depth to the discussion about what this has meant from a general media standpoint, and Chapter 5 discusses some of the legal issues with social media bans throughout the world but, in general, social media allows for instantaneous communication across borders in ways that have been unimaginable until the last generation. It is possible to witness the destructive natural disasters that have taken place all over the globe in real-time, while a simple swipe brings the user into an English Premier League football match, another to a political protest, another to an LIV or PGA Golf tournament, and another to a major tennis event, and then back to a Major League Baseball game, all with the ability for the user to comment on these events and communicates with billions of others.

This reality speaks to the rapid power and development of communications technologies and an interconnected, interdependent world (Schwanen, 2018). Stephen Wagg and David Andrews have argued that "culture became a vehicle through which – in the absence of more conventional forms and frequencies of military engagement – the competing communist and capitalist orders sought to assert their civil, ideological, and moral ascendancy" (2007, p. 2) and, as such, national identity has been largely reduced to a relic with cultural importance, but whose borders matter less in the digital age than in previous historical epochs. George Ritzer (2019) suggests that social media has allowed for the expansion of *calculability, datafication, self-tracking*, and the turning of consumers into *prosumers* in nearly infinite ways. Many applications and other social media sites allow for our personal information, data, and consumer behavior to be tracked and influenced, in ways that further shape global production of goods, services, as well as the delivery and experiences of sport spectacles (Oliver, 2022).

Much like class, race, and gender/sexuality, nationalism and globalization play out in social mediascapes in ways that are exciting and dangerous. Yes, social movements can be organized and carried on globally, but they can be done so in ways that serve social justice (Harvey et al., 2013) – like work done to bring safe drinking water to poor populations by global corporations (Bunds, 2017) – or allow for cross-cultural, transnational racism to exist (Kilvington & Price, 2019). Perhaps the most disarming aspect of globalized social media movements in and around sports is that national laws, which Chapter 5 already demonstrated are relatively easy to navigate for unscrupulous social media users, are even more confounded when abusers and bullies do not even live in the country of the person they are threatening to or actually (digitally) attacking. In sum, modern globalization that is driven by social media is a brave new world where there is much opportunity for good and malice.

Case 6.4 Formula 1 Explodes as a Global Phenomenon With the Help of Social Media

Formula 1 has long been a truly global sport, with racers and fans hailing from a variety of locales. However, it has often been cast as a secondary or "niche" sport when compared to the likes of soccer or basketball. Driven, in part, by the popularity of the Netflix show *Drive to Survive* (2019–present) and the thirst of general sport fans to watch any live programming during the COVID pandemic, the sport has skyrocketed in popularity. Official audience figures measuring seven major global markets show that 1.5 billion people comprised the television audience in 2020, and that several highly populated countries including Russia, China, the Netherlands, the UK, Germany, and the United States saw growth in viewership.

Given the global nature of F1 events and the exorbitant costs to obtain a spectator pass, parking, and lodging, most fans have never actually attended a live race. However, the sport has strengthened its social media presence across numerous platforms such as Facebook, X, YouTube, Snapchat, TikTok, Twitch, and Chinese social media platforms to realize a 35% increase in followers, and the largest engagement growth across all major sport leagues in the world (Ghorpade, 2021). More recently, a survey conducted by Nielsen and Motorsport Network found that the fan base is becoming more diverse (women viewership doubled), and that fans were not only following F1 but also its racers via social media. In sum, the sport took advantage of the COVID pandemic to increase its global reach largely with the benefit of social media.

Sources: www.sportskeeda.com/f1/news-how-formula-1-became-world-s-engaging-sport

www.formula1.com/en/latest/article.formula-1-reveals-details-of-fan-segmentation-research.19u9fkhcB8cOoclwAacuow.html#:~:text=The%20survey%20then%20identified%20groups%20branded%20%E2%80%98Sociables%E2%80%99%2C%20who,as%20being%20more%20in%20tune%20with%20their%20needs.

www.sportschangers.com/sports/the-formula-1-audience-who-and-where-are-the-fans/

Social Media and the Democratization of Representation

In review, social media has great power and the possibility for positive social change in and through sport. Yet, it does not do so in a completely free and safe manner. If anyone can have access to and produce content without a moral and ethical governor, then just about anything goes on social media. Some of the anything that takes place is downright vicious and makes participation in the digital world fraught with peril for marginalized communities across class, race, gender, sexual, and global sites. This does not have to be the case.

As this chapter has outlined, there are numerous sporting examples for how social media can provide a safe haven for multitudes of underserved individuals to communicate their conditions of inequity by providing evidence for and community to commiserate with as the crushing power of a racist, sexist, homo- and trans-phobic society rallies against them. The possibilities for movement towards a more peaceful and socially just society driven by social media platforms are there but require the support from those coming from privilege to achieve it.

More to the point, social media to reach users and help effectuate change in and through sport are there. Sport managers of social media platforms for F1, the LGBTQ+ community, and those looking to "kick racism out" of soccer/football have been able to develop platforms for the voices of others to be heard. It is very likely that progress can be made in helping these individuals and communities centered on sport to live better lives through social media, and to provide hope for a better tomorrow.

Note

1 The authors would like to acknowledge that the term "Redskin" is a dated racist term that was permitted to exist in professional sports for far too long. It is not lost on the authors that this term may be hurtful/harmful to some readers, but was used for accuracy in the example.

References

Adams, M. (2011). *Artistic impressions: Figure skating, masculinity, and the limits of sport*. Toronto, ON: University of Toronto Press.

Alderman, D., Inwood, J., & Tyner, J. (2018). Jack Johnson versus Jim Crow: Race, reputation, and the politics of black villainy: The Fight of the century. *Southeastern Geographer, 58*(3), 227–249.

Antunovic, D., & Linden, A. (2015). Disrupting dominant discourses: #HERESPROOF of interest in women's sports. *Feminist Media Studies, 15*(1), 157–159.

Associated Press (2023a). Germany under-17 national team racially abused on way to winning European title. *AP News*. https://apnews.com/article/germany-u17-soccer-racism-1d1259c6956ab6b669424ccce8c70e8f

Associated Press (2023b). German soccer players face racist abuse on social media at U21 European Championship. *AP News*. https://apnews.com/article/germany-racism-european-u21-championship-a5540152e1a64f8ce306f49acb97fdc4

Azzarito, L., & Harrison, Jr., L. (2008). 'White men can't jump': Race, gender and natural athleticism. *International Review for the Sociology of Sport, 43*(4), 347–364.

Baker, S., & Rowe, D. (2013). The Power of popular publicity: New social media and the affective dynamics of the sport racism scandal. *Journal of Political Power, 6*(3), 441–460.

Bilas, J. (2022). Why NIL has been good for college sports ... and the hurdels that remain. *ESPN.com*. Accessed April 25, 2023 from https://www.espn.com/college-sports/story/_/id/34161311/why-nil-good-college-sports-hurdles-remain

Blinder, A., Hirsch, L., & Draper, K. (2023). How the PGA tour's deal with the Saudi wealth fund could collapse. *New York Times*. www.nytimes.com/2023/06/27/sports/golf/pga-tour-liv-golf-merger-obstacles.html

Braude, J. (2020). Howard Bryant on the need for 'dissidence' in fighting systemic racism. *GBH News*. Accessed April 21, 2023 from https://www.youtube.com/watch?v=bCMMyug7Ni0&t=6s

Bunds, K. (2017). *Sport, politics and the charity industry: Running for water*. London: Routledge.

Boykoff, J. (2022). Toward a theory of sportswashing: Mega-events, soft power, and political conflict. *Sociology of Sport Journal, 39*(4), 342–351.

Bourdieu, P. (1984). *Distinction: A Social critique of the judgment of taste*. Cambridge, MA: Harvard University Press.

Bourdieu, P. (1997). The forms of capital. In A. Halsey, H. Lauder, P. Brown & A. Stuart Wells (Eds.). *Education: Culture, economy, and society* (pp. 46–58). Oxford, England: Oxford University Press.

Carpenter, J. (2023). Norman among highest LIV gainers on social; Mickelson down the most. *Sport Business Journal*. Retrieved July 10, 2023 from https://www.sportsbusinessjournal.com/Daily/Issues/2023/04/24/Media/liv-golf-social-media-data.aspx

Cassidy, W. (2017). Inching away from the toy department: Daily newspaper sports vocerage of Jason Collins' and Michael Sam's coming out. *Communication & Sport*, 5(5), 534–553.

Cleland, J. (2014). Racism, football fans, and online message boards: How social media has added a new dimension to racist discourse in English football. *Journal of Sport and Social Issues*, 38(5), 415–431.

Dann, L., & Everbach, T. (2016). Opening the sports closet: Media coverage of the self-outings of Jason Collins and Brittney Griner. *Journal of Sports Media*, 11(1), 169–192.

De Ridder, S., & Van Bauwel, S. (2015). The Discursive construction of gay teenagers in times of mediatization: Youth's reflections on intimate storytelling, queer shame and realness in popular social media places. *Journal of Youth Studies*, 18(6), 777–793.

Drive to Survive: Formula 1. (2023). Netflix original series.

Duello, T., Rivedal, S., Wickland, C., & Weller, A. (2021). Race and genetics versus 'race in genetics. A Systematic review of the use of African ancestry in genetic studies. *Evolution, Medicine & Public Health*, 9(1), 232–245.

Ehrenreich, B. (2021). *Nickel and dimed: On (not) getting by in America*. New York: Henry Holt and Company.

Farrington, N., Hall, L., Kilvington, D., Price, J., & Said, A. (2015). *Sport, racism and social media*. London: Routledge.

Filo, K., Lock, D., & Karg, A. (2015). Sport and social media research: A Review. *Sport Management Review*, 18(2), 166–181.

Fraser, O. (2022). Trans swimmer Lia Thomas opens up about social media hate. *GCN*. Accessed April 25, 2023 from https://gcn.ie/lia-thomas-response/

Furstenau, M. (2022). Racism in Germany is part of everyday life. *DW*. www.dw.com/en/racism-in-germany-is-part-of-everyday-life/a-61700339

Ghorpade, N. (2021). How Formula 1 became the world's most engaging sport. *Sportskeeda*. www.sportskeeda.com/f1/news-how-formula-1-became-world-s-engaging-sport

Hamel, R. (2023). LIV golf is putting its events back on YouTube – But you're going to have to pay for it. *USA Today*. www.usatoday.com/story/sports/golf/2023/05/26/liv-golf-on-youtube-cost/51525471/

Harvey, D. (1999). Time-space compression and the postmodern condition. In M. Waters (ed.) *Modernity critical concepts* (pp. 98–118). London: Routledge.

Harvey, J., Horne, J., Safai, P., Courchesne-O'Neill, S., & Darnell, S. (2013). *Sport and social movements: From the local to the global*. New York: Bloomsbury Academic.

Hylton, K., & Lawrence, S. (2016). "For your ears only!" Donald Sterling and backstage racism in sport. *Ethnic and Racial Studies*, 39(15), 2740–2757.

Jackson, J., Weidman, N., & Rubin, G. (2005). The origins of scientific racism. *The Journal of Blacks in Higher Education*, 50(50), 66–79.

Jane, E. (2014). "You're a ugly, whorish, slut": Understanding e-bile. *Feminist Media Studies*, 14(4), 531–546.

King-White, R. (2013). I am not a scientist: Being honest with oneself and the researched in critical interventionist ethnography. *Sociology of Sport Journal*, 30(3), 296–322.

King-White, R. (2022). "I didn't ask for any of this": (White) privilege, the American (dream) family, and health care. *Cultural StudiesóCritical Methodologies*, 22(5), 533–543.

King-White, R., & Giardina, M. (2023). Parenting in pandemic times: Notes on the emotional geography of youth sport culture. In. D. Andrews, H. Thorpe & J. Newman (Eds.) *Sport and Physical Culture in Global Pandemic Times: COVID Assemblages* (pp. 445–469). Cham: Springer International Publishing.

Kilvington, D., & Price, J. (2019). Tackling social media abuse? Critically assessing English football's response to online racism. *Communication & Sport, 7*(1), 64–79.

Krieger, N. (2000). Refiguring "race": Epidemiology, racialized biology, and biological expressions of race relations. *International Journal of Health Services, 30*(1), 211–216.

Leeds, M., & Rockoff, H. (2019). Beating the odds: Black jockeys in the Kentucky Derby, 1870–1911. In J. Wilson and R. Pomfret (Eds.) *Historical perspectives on sports economics: Lessons from the field* (pp. 136–149). Cheltenham, UK: Edward Elgar Publishing.

Leitch, W. (2015). Nobody cares if you lie. *Deadspin*. April 21, 2023 from https://deadspin.com/nobody-cares-if-you-lie-1750284878

Levin, J., & Stahl, J. (2014). Who's behind the new Washington football team website. *Slate*. Retrieved April 24, 2023 from https://slate.com/culture/2014/07/the-washington-nfl-team-wants-you-to-think-there-s-a-grass-roots-movement-in-support-of-its-offensive-nickname-is-there-really.html

Love, A., Deeb, A., & Waller, S. (2019). Social justice, sport and racism: A Position statement. *Quest, 71*(2), 227–238.

Lucas, C., & Hodler, M. (2018). #Takebackfitspo: Building queer futures in/through social media. In K. Toffoletti, H. Thorpe, J. Francombe-Webb (eds.) *New Sporting femininities: Embodied politics in postfeminist times* (pp. 231–251). Cham, Switzerland: Palgrave Macmillan.

Maier, P. (1999). The Strange history of "all men are created equal". *Washington and Less Law Review, 56*(3), 873–888.

McRae, D. (2014). *In Black and white: The Untold story of Joe Louis and Jesse Owens*. New York: Simon & Schuster.

Meyerowitz, J. (2004). *How sex changed: A History of transsexuality in the United States*. Cambridge, MA: Harvard University Press.

Millard, D. (2023). *How golf can save your life*. New York: Abrams Books.

Muller-Wille, S. (2014). Race and history: Comments from an epistemological point of view. *Science, Technology & Human Values, 39*(4), 597–606.

Oliver, J. (2022). Data brokers: Last week tonight with John Oliver. Accessed April 25, 2023 from https://www.youtube.com/watch?v=wqn3gR1WTcA

Oshiro, K., Weems, A., & Singer, J. (2021). Cyber racism toward black athletes: A Critical race analysis of TexAgs.com online brand community. *Communication & Sport, 9*(6), 911–933.

Parry, K., & Magrath, R. (2022). Social media, digital technology, and sexuality in sport. *Emerald Insight*. www.emerald.com/insight/content/doi/10.1108/S1476-28542 0220000015016/full/html

Petchesky, B. (2014). New, "grassroots" pro-Redskins website is run by a pr firm, of course. *Deadspin*. Retrieved April 24, 2023 from https://deadspin.com/new-grassroots-pro-redskins-website-is-run-by-a-pr-f-1613362975

Phillips, J., & Phillips, P. (1993). History from below: Women's underwear and the rise of women's sport. *Journal of Popular Culture, 27*(2), 129–148.

Rampton, M. (2015). Four waves of feminism. *Pacific University Oregon, 25*, 1–10.

Rampton, M. (2019). Four waves of feminism. *Pacific Magazine*. Accessed April 25, 2023 from http://gdelaurier.pbworks.com/w/file/fetch/134554611/Four%20Waves%20of%20Feminism%20_%20Pacific%20University.pdf

Ritzer, G. (2019). *The McDonaldization of society into the digital age*. London: Sage.

Sage, G. (1993). Sport and physical education and the new world order: Dare we be agents of social change. *Quest, 45*(2), 151–164.

Schwanen, T. (2018). Thinking complex interconnections: Transition, nexus and geography. *Transactions of the Institute of British Geographers, 43*(2), 262–283.

Sharrow, E. Tarsi, M., & Nteta, T. (2021). What's in a name? Symbolic racism, public opinion, and the controversy over the NFL's Washington football team name. *Race and Social Problems, 13,* 110–121.

Stewart, J. (2014). The Redskins name – Catching racism. *The Daily Show with John Stewart*. Retrieved April 24, 2023 from https://www.cc.com/video/189afv/the-daily-show-with-jon-stewart-the-redskins-name-catching-racism

Staurowsky, E. (ed.) (2016). *Women and sport: Continuing a journey of liberation and celebration*. Champaign, IL: Human Kinetics.

Vann, P. (2014). Changing the game: The Role of social media in overcoming old media's attention deficit toward women's sport. *Journal of Broadcasting & Electronic Media, 58*(3), 438–455.

Wagg, S., & Andrews, D. (2007). *East plays west: Sport and the cold war*. London: Routledge.

Weiller, K., & Higgs, C. (1994). The All-American Girls Professional Baseball League, 1943-1954: Gender conflict in sport? *Sociology of Sport Journal, 11*(3), 289–297.

Weiner, D. (2023). Women's NCAA tournament tv ratings are through the roof. *Bleacher Report*. Accessed April 25, 2023 from https://www.bleachernation.com/news/2023/03/22/womens-ncaa-tournament-tv-ratings-are-through-the-roof/

Yates, S., & Lockley, E. (2018). Social media and social class. *American Behavioral Scientist, 629,* 1291–1316.

Index

Note: Numbers in *italics* and **bold** indicate figures and tables, respectively.

30 for 30 (documentary) 59

abuse 76; reporting mechanisms, clarity (absence) 76
abusive user account, locking 73
activation, success (increase) 27
ad space, Redskins payment 86
adults/children, power imbalances 76
advanced tools/technologies, adoption 37, 41–42
advertising, fostering 39
Africa, social media (case study) **60**
All-American Girls Professional: Baseball League, women (participation) 93
allyship, social media space 95
alternative viewpoints (sharing), space (providing) 84
Alvarez, Canela (product/service endorsement) 30–31
amateurism, sports (relationship) 89
ambassador, role/function 31–32
ambush marketing 20; evolution 30; impact 28–29; marketing objectives, implementation 21; social media, relationship 28–30; sport media, importance 9; strategies, evolution 30; techniques, categories 29–30
analytics, usage 50, 52
Andreescu, Bianca Vanessa (co-presentational endorsement mode) 32
anti-racism, social media (relationship) 91
artificial intelligence (AI), usage (trend) 17
associative ambushing 30

athletes: account, product advocacy 31; ambassador role 31–32; celebrity athletes, social media platform usage 31–32; college athletes (company representative) 71–72; discrimination, encounter 12; platform, public awareness (raising) 12; public scrutiny/intrusion 15; risk 73–74; social media, positive space 75; student-athletes, discipline 71
athletics, space 72–73; LGBTQ+ participants 94
audience: engagement (social media management) 50; global audience, understanding **51**; groups, characteristics/needs (understanding) 44; personalization 44; segmentation 44; trust, development 50
Australia, death threat (control) (case study) **75**
authentic interaction 51
authenticity, importance 50, 51
Avon (implicit endorsement mode) 32
awareness: building 11; creation, goal 27

Barstool (blog) 59–61
Barstool Sports (social media site) 78, 94
Bartoli, Maron (physical threats) 77
Basketball Africa League (BAL) 60
Benzema, Karim (sexual maltreatment) (case study) **78**
bias (social media challenges) 15

biological sex identification 92
blacks, sport participation (allowance) 89
Blake, Jacob (racist killing) 91
Bleacher Report (blog) 59
blogs: future 58–60; social media platform classification 6; usage 2
Bollea, Terry (Hulk Hogan) lawsuit (case study) **78–79**
Bolt, Usain (imperative endorsement mode) 23
Boston Sports Guy blog (Simmons) 59
Bourdieu, Pierre 85
brand: associations 24, 25; associations (Manchester United) **25**; elements, interaction (usage) 25; humanization 34; identities 31; loyalty 25; loyalty (Manchester United) **26**; perceived brand quality 24; personalities, usage 26; promotion 1; social media, relationship 23–25
brand awareness 24; case study 25–26; raising 21, 42, 46, 48
brand awareness (Manchester United) **25**
brand equity: components 24–25; defining 24; enjoyment 24; increase/boost 24, 25
branding 20; consistency **52**; marketing objectives, implementation 21
brand management: components 24–25; fostering 39; goal 24; social media, importance/value 9, 24; sport brand management 20, 23, 25
Bryant, Kobe (brand association) 24
budgets, determination 46
burner, creation 73
Burn It All Down (podcast) 91
business: goals, accomplishment 48; objectives, social media (integration) 42; pages, emergency 39; social media presence 39; value, recognition 39

calculability, expansion 96–97
call-to-action buttons, usage 46
campaigns, success (gauging) 45
cave art, appearance 54
celebrity athletes, social media platform usage 31–32
Celtics (brand association) 24
Chicago Blackhawks: fan connection **44–45**; X strategy, engagement **44–45**

child-athlete, coach (power imbalance) 77
children: adults, power imbalances 76; athletes, risk 73–74
child sexual abuse (CSA) 76–77; study 77
Chinese sport social media, Tencent (relationship) **57**
class matters 86–87
click-through rates (KPI element) 45
coach, child-athlete (power imbalance) 77
coattail ambushing 29–30
collaborative relationships, building 33–34
college athletes (company representative) 71–72
college campuses, safe spaces 84
Collins, Jason (homosexuality) 94
communication: ability 54; direct line 22; process 33–34; usage 35
community interaction, encouragement 47
community management 48; online community management 43, 47; process 47
companies: humanization 26; pages, creation 39
Comtois, Maxime (sexual media abuse) (case study) **79**
connectivity 26
Consensus Statement on Sexual Harassment and Abuse in Sport (IOC) 73–74, 76; update, case study **74**
content communities: description 6–7; examples 7; social media platform classification 6; usage 2
content creation 43–44; strategizing **51**
content curation 43–44
content strategy, creation 50
contracts 13
conversation: forum, creation 12; loyal follower engagement 8; onlooker engagement, rarity 8
conversion rates (KPI element) 45
conversions (social media metric) 42
co-presentational endorsement mode 32
copyright infringements 13
Corpus, The (blog) 59
COVID-19: impact 53; live programming, need **97**; social media, relationship 95; spread 93
crisis communication 14
crisis-response planning 14
Crypto.com 25, 27
cryptocurrency platform, usage 27
cultural capital, social class function 85

cultural norms, abuse (normalization) 76
Curry, Stephen: product/service endorsement 30–31; X photo 32
customer care **51**
customer experience-related issues 23
customer service 20; fostering 39; marketing objectives, implementation 21; social media, relationship 22–23
customer-valued product, production/ delivery 33–34
cyberbullying 13; Japanese Olympic team, relationship (case study) **69**; possibility 15; social media challenges 15; victims 80
cyber-stalking, arrests 75

Dan LeBatard Show with Stugotz, The (radio show) 61
data: analytics, usage (trend) 17; privacy (social media challenges) 14–15
data-driven approach, usage 48
data-driven decision making 47; business emphasis 37
data-driven social media management 43, 45; focus 42
datafication, expansion 96–97
Deadspin (blog) 59–61, 73; early versions 94
death threats, New Zealand/Australia (impact) (case study) **75**
defamation (social media challenges) 13, 14
Defector (blog) 59–61, 73, 91
defining characteristics 1; social media 7–8; social media users 7–8
destructive natural disasters, witnessing 96
devotees (social media user category) 8
digital content, user access 6
direct customer service, assistance 22–23
discrimination: encounter 12; facilitation 76; forms 11, 77; LGBTQ+ discrimination 11; racial discrimination, experiences 88
discussion sites: examples 7; range 7; social media platform classification 6; usage 2
diversity: endeavors 14; initiatives 15; issues 1; issues, awareness (promotion) 12; promotion 12; social media 12–13; sport 12–13; support 13; value, emphasis 12

Draft Kings contract 61
Drasanvi (explicit endorsement mode) 32
Dr. Dre (Heineken appearance) **40**
drive sales, fostering 39
Drive to Survive (show) 97
Drone Racing League (DRL), social media usage **10–11**
Durant, Kevin ("Dream Fearlessly") 32
dynamic content, usage 44

e-bile 77, 94
e-commerce channels, significance 3
economic capital, social class function 85
economic drivers 2–3
Edge of Sports (blog) 59, 91
elite athletes, risk 73–74
emotional health issues (social media challenges) 89
Emotional maltreatment 79
emotional violence 80
End of Sports, The (podcast) 91
endorsement 20; attraction 33; communication 31; marketing objectives, implementation 21; modes 32; purpose 31; social media, relationship 30–32
engagement: driving **51**; KPI element 45; rate (social media metric) 42, 52
equal rights, promotion 95
ESPN: airing, initiation 55; liberal agenda, perception 71
esports, sexual harassment (presence) 75–76
even playing field space, perception 75–76
explicit endorsement mode 32

Facebook: Ads, usage 46; group, creation 25; introduction 5; launch 4; multi-way conversations, engagement 2; usage 24
familial/friend group connectivity 67
fan behavior, impropriety 15
fan-centric content marketing **41**
fan engagement: sport media, importance 9
fan groups, emergence 10
faux privacy 68
Favre, Brett: misogyny, case study **78–79**; sexual harassment allegation 59
FC Barcelona: adaptability **52**; analysis/optimization, usage **52**; authentic interaction, importance **51**; branding,

consistency **52**; community building **51**; content creation, strategizing **51**; customer care **51**; engagement, driving **51**; fan engagement, social media (leveraging) **51–52**; global audience, understanding **51**; objectives, defining **51**; social media approach, authenticity (importance) **51–52**; visual appeal, leveraging **51**
Fédération Internationale de Football Association (FIFA) 23, 29
feedback, space (social media provision) 67
femininity, proof 93
Fire Joe Morgan (blog) 59
First Amendment (US Constitution) 68
first-wave feminism 92
first-wave feminists, socio-political advancements 93
Flickr, launch 5
Ford, congratulatory message (property infringement) 29
Formula 1 (global phenomenon), social media (impact) **97–98**
France, soccer sex tape lawsuit **78**
Freedom House report 68
freedom of expression, space 72
free speech, social media (relationship) 6
Friendster, launch 4
funnel-based focus groups, usage 34

Garner, Eric (racist killing) 91
Gawker, lawsuit (case study) **78–79**
gender: fluidity 93; tripartite conceptualization 92
gender-neutral pronouns, usage 12–13
gender/sexuality 97; divisions, undermining 85; social media, relationship 92–96
German Center for Integration and Migration Research (DeZIM), media analysis 90
German soccer, racism (relationship) (case study) **90**
global audience, understanding **51**
global brand building, narrative (usage) **41**
globalization, social media (relationship) 96–97
God Bless Football (podcast) 61
Good Rivals, The (film) 62
goodwill effect 26
graphic design, impact 27

Griner, Brittney: homosexuality 94; social media, usage **95**

harassment 73; sexual harassment 75–76; social media challenges 15; victims 80
hashtags: tracking 46; usage 27
health: race, connection 88–89; racial/ethnic inequalities 88
Heineken, Lomu/McCaw/Dr. Dre appearances **40**
Hi5, launch 5
highlight packages, creation, social media provision 67
Highly Questionable (television show) 61
high school athletes (company representative) 71
Hill, Jemele (company representative) 70–71
His & Hers 70
homophobia 11–12
human blueprint, understanding 88
Human Genome Project (HGP) 88–90
hypermasculine "sport bro," market (presence) 73

ideas (marketplace), freedom of expression (space) 72
imperative endorsement mode 32
implicit endorsement mode 32
impressions (social media metric) 42
inclusion: endeavors 14; increase, campaign 11–12; initiatives 15; issues 1; male challenge 94; promotion 12; social media/sport 12–13; support 13; value, emphasis 12
inclusive culture (importance), awareness (increase) 12
influencers: endeavors 46; James, impact 33; marketing 21, 39, 43, 46; partnerships 44; social media influencers 16, 17, 72; social media user category 8; top-tier social media users 8; YouTube 86
informal social media management 39
information: breaches 14–15; flow 29; sharing 4, 68
Instagram: Ads, usage 46; content community example 7; introduction 5; Paul post 32; usage 2, 24
integration, success 41

intellectual property 13
interaction: approach, importance 45; authentic interaction 51; community interaction, encouragement 47; encouragement 50; forum, creation 12; process 33–34; social media purposes 34; usage 25, 34–35; *see also* social interaction
International Olympic Committee (IOC) 29–30; Consensus Statement on Sexual Harassment and Abuse in Sport 73–74, 76; Consensus Statement on Sexual Harassment and Abuse in Sport, update (case study) **74**
Internet: applications, multi-way conversations (engagement) 2; connectivity 86; future 58–60; high-speed Internet access, expansion 16; impact 2

James, LeBron 23; endorsements **33**; influencer, impact **33**; Nike Air Zoom Generation 1, tweet 31; product/service endorsement 30–31; social media presence, harnessing **33**
Japanese Olympic Committee (JOC), accounts monitoring **69**
Japanese Olympic team, cyberbullying (relationship) (case study) **69**
Jim Brockmire Show, the (podcast) 62
Jorgensen, Christine (hormonal therapy) 92
Junior Tour Powered by Under Armour (UAJT), case study **63–64**

Kaepernick, Colin (protest) 70
key performance indicators (KPIs) 45; setup 47–48
keywords, tracking 46
Kick It Out **79**
Kimes, Mina 61; ESPN role 93
Kissing Suzy Kolber (blog) 59, 94

labor strife, pro-management opinions (promotion) 56
Laker Nation (brand association) 24
Lakers, social media profile 24
language: coalescence 54; power 12–13
Latin American, social media/sport (case study) **56**

League of Their Own, A (film) 93
leagues, social media functions 9
Legacy: The True Story of the LA Lakers (documentary) 25
legal/ethical issues, social media (relationship) 67
lesbian/gay/bisexual/trans-sexual (LGBT) athletes, risk 73–74
LGBTQ+: community 94; discrimination 11; social media, space (safety) 95–96
#LGTBQRIGHTS (social media catch-all) 95
LinkedIn: Ads, usage 46; introduction 5; launch 4
link, piggybacking 30
LiveJournal (social networking websites) 4
live streaming, trend 16
LIV Golf, social media (relationship) (case study) **87**
local community sport organizations, social media usage 20–21
Lomu, Jonah (Heineken campaign appearance) **40**
long-term relationship: development 33–34; enhancement 35; maintenance 16, 35
long-term success, audience trust (development) 50
Los Angeles (brand association) 24
loyal followers, conversation engagement 8
loyalty, display 25
lurkers (social media user category) 8

major sporting events, coverage (rights fees) 64
major sport leagues, engagement growth 97–98
male-dominated spaces, challenge 94
maltreatment: emotional maltreatment 79; physical maltreatment 77; presence 77–79; sexual maltreatment 77–78
Manchester United: brand associations **25**; brand awareness **25**; brand loyalty **26**; brand (building), social media (usage) **25–26**; perceived brand quality **26**
marginalized sub-cultures (study), social media (usage) 91
marketing strategy, social media (integration) **40–41**

Martin, Trayvon (racist killing) 91
McCaw, Richie (Heineken campaign appearance) **40**
Meadowlark (catalog) 91
Meadowlarkers (podcast) 61–62
Meadowlark Media 84; formation 61–62
media: members, company representative role 69–79; (re)presenters, identification 55–56; sport, relationship 54–56
men, equality (belief) 88, 92
mental health issues (social media challenges) 15
mental superiority, space (sports provision) 89
mental well-being, toll 15
mentions, tracking 46
Michelin, associative ambushing 30
Mike and the Mad Dog (WFAN) 58
minglers (social media user category) 8
minorities, sport participation (allowance) 89
minority (niche) sports, social media (importance) 9–10
misinformation: social media challenges 14; spreading 68
mobile optimization, trend 16
mobile-responsive interfaces, creation 16
monitoring: social monitoring 46–47; solutions 47; tools, usage 50
multinational companies, friendships 37
multi-way conversations, engagement 2
Murray, Andy (physical threats) 77
MySpace, launch 4
mythologies, spreading 68

Nadal, Rafael (explicit endorsement mode) 32
Name Image and Likeness (NIL): compensation, earning right 72; revision 96
National Collegiate Athletic Association (NCAA), student-athletes (employee viewpoint) 72
national/global divisions, undermining 85
nationalism, social media (relationship) 96–97
NBA championships (brand association) 24
NBC, coattail ambushing 29–30
newbies: social media user category 8; social media users, equivalence 8
New Zealand All Blacks: fan-centric content marketing **41**; global brand building, narrative (usage) **41**; marketing strategy, social media integration **40–41**; social brand, boundaries (extension) **40**
New Zealand, death threat control (case study) **75**
Nike Air Zoom Generation 1 (James tweet) 31
Nolan, Katie (ESPN role) 93
non-direct communication 77
non-heterosexual athletes, sports participation **94–95**
non-sponsoring firms, creative strategies 28–29
Numbers Never Lie 70

objectives, defining **51**
observer, athlete role 32
Office, The 59
official sponsors, ambush marketing (impact) 28–29
Off the Looking Glass (podcast) 61
OmnicomMediaGroup (OMG) study 56
on-court sporting performances, attention 96
on-field sporting performances, attention 96
online abuse (social media challenges) 15
online communities: building 4; emergence 10; formation 3; hubs 47; involvement 21
online community management 47
online resources, public availability 2
online video game competitions, even playing field space (perception) 75–76
onlookers: conversation engagement, rarity 8; social media user category 8
on-pitch sporting performances, attention 96
organizations, social media usage 12
outcomes, evaluation (social media management) 50
outness 95

paid advertising (social media management) 46
para-sports, visibility (promotion) 12
Parks and Recreation 59
participatory social media 26–28
patriarchal hierarchy, challenge 92–93

Index

patriarchal society, considerations 92
Paul, Chris (Instagram post) 32
pejorative terminology, avoidance 12–13
perceived brand quality 24
perceived brand quality (Manchester United) 26
personalization 44
personifier, athlete role 32
physical maltreatment 77
physical superiority, space (sports provision) 89
Pinterest: content community example 7; introduction 5
Pirelli, values ambushing 29
platform-specific expertise 48
platform-specific knowledge 48
podcasts, future 61–62
positive social change, promotion 91
power: imbalances 76; structure, fissures 92
pressure (social media challenges) 15
privacy 13; absence, social media challenges 15; faux privacy 68; threat, social media (impact) 13
product, athlete advocacy 31
property: direct affiliation, establishment 29–30; infringement 29–30
prosumers, consumer shift 96–97
public awareness, increase 29
public forum 26
public relations, fostering 39
Puma (imperative endorsement mode) 32
PyeongChang Games, Michelin (associative ambushing) 30

QAnon, conspiratorial posts 68
Quora (discussion site example) 7

race: characteristics, reification 89; health/social class, connection 88–89; social construct 88; social media, relationship 88–91; sport, relationship 89
racial discrimination, experiences 88
racial/ethnic inequalities 88
racism: expulsion 98; German soccer, relationship (case study) **90**; social media, relationship 90–91
racist society, existence **90**
racist views, publication/sharing 91
radio, future 58
Raisman, Aly (coattail ambushing) 30
reach (KPI element) 45
Real Madrid, followers 24

real-time customer service, assistance 22–23
real-time functionality 26
real-time updates 14
real-world concerns, space (contrast) 76
Reckoning Always Comes, The (article) 73
Reddit: discussion site example 7; introduction 5
"Redskins Facts" (support group) 86
relational ties, user list (social media platform attribute) 6
relationship: management 46; success 33
relationship marketing 20; approach 33–34; goals 33; marketing objectives, implementation 21; social media, connection 33–35; sport media, importance 9; tool 34; value, creation 35
religion, socio-cultural issue 12
representation: democratization, social media (relationship) 98; increase, campaign 11–12; social media challenges 15
reputation management 14
return on investment (ROI), determination 46
revenue generation: sport media, importance 9
reverse racists, impact 91
Rio Games, Subway (X usage) 29–30
Ronaldo, Cristiano 24; Instagram account, content community example 7; product/service endorsement 30; Snapchat, content community example 7
Rooney, Wayne (physical threats) 77
rumor, spread 79
Russo, Christopher "Mad Dog" 58

safe spaces 84
sales management: sport media, importance 9
sales, marketing objectives (implementation) 21
Salisbury, Sean (misogyny) (case study) **78–79**
Sam, Michael (homosexuality) 94
Sanchez, Mark (physical threats) 77
Saturday Night Live 59
scheduling, space (social media provision) 67

Schilling, Curt 71; media representative 70; social media presence, messaging problems 70
security (social media challenges) 14–15
segmentation 44
self-tracking, expansion 96–97
semi-structured interviews 34
sex: fluidity 93; sex-change operations 92; tripartite conceptualization 92
sexual harassment 75–76
sexualities: alternatives 92; fluidity 93
sexuality: tripartite conceptualization 92; Western World, relationship **94–95**
sexual maltreatment 77–78
sexual media abuse (Comtois) (case study) **79**
sexual violence 80; threats 78, 94
Sharapova, Maria (implicit endorsement mode) 32
shared updates, creation 39
sincerity, importance 50
Six Degrees (social networking websites) 4; introduction 5
SnapChat: content community example 7; impact 76–77; introduction 5
snaps, usage 5
soccer clubs (Europe), social media trends **62–63**
social brand, boundaries (extension) **40**
social capital, social class function 85
social class: continuum 86; distinctions 89; race, connection 88–89; reification 85; social media, relationship 85–87; understanding 85
social commerce: online communities, involvement 21; social media, relationship 21–22; usage, trend 17
social drivers 2–3
social hub, build-in ability 26
social interaction: engagement 8; possibilities, creation 3; principles 2
social issues 84; awareness, mobilizing/raising 3
social justice warriors, impact 91
social listening 46–47; involvement 43; process 47; social media platform 39; solutions, aid 47
social media: abusive user account, locking 73; advanced tools/technologies, adoption 41–42; Africa, case study **60**; ambush marketing, relationship 28–30; ambush marketing techniques, categories 29–30; anti-racism, relationship 91; business objectives, integration 42; business pages, emergency 39; business value, recognition 39; campaigns (success), evaluation (KPI setup) 48; challenges 14–15; communication 77; cultural acceleration 67; customer service, relationship 22–23; death threats, New Zealand/Australia (impact) (case study) **75**; defining 2; defining characteristics 7–8; departments, impact 42; diversity 12–13; early individual adoption 37–39; economic benefits 3; efforts (success measurement), analytics (usage) 52; emergence 3–6; endorsements, personal nature 31; endorsements, relationship 30–32; evolution 14; expansion 1–3; free speech, relationship 68; functions 9; future 16–17, 56–64; future, trends **16**; gender/sexuality, relationship 92–96; global growth, factors 2–3; globalization, relationship 96–97; global perspective 62; growth 3–6; impact **97–98**; inclusion 12–13; influencers 16, 17, 72; informal social media management 39; initiatives, impact 42; integration 40; interaction, usage/purpose 34; issues 84; Latin America, case study **56**; lawsuit (US), case study **78–79**; legal/ethical issues, relationship 67; legal issues, future 80; LIV Golf, relationship (case study) **87**; loyalty, display 25; maltreatment, presence 77–79; marginalized sub-cultures, relationship 91; marketing efforts (success evaluation), analytics/monitoring tools

(usage) 50; nationalism, relationship 96–97; objectives 48, 50; participatory social media 26–28; pathways 84–85; power 7–8; race, relationship 88–91; racism, relationship 90–91; realm 89; relationship marketing, connection 33–35; role, relationship marketing tool 34; significance 1; social class, relationship 85–87; social commerce, relationship 21–22; sponsorship, relationship 26–28; sport business management, relationship 9–10; sport business, relationship 20; sport, crisis communication 14; sport, emerging issues 9–14; sport, legal issues 13; sport, socio-cultural issues 11–12; term, usage 6; traditional media, relationship 53; trends (European soccer clubs) **62–63**; unique characteristics 30; usage (Manchester United) **25–26**; usage, transformations 37–42, *38*; use, elements 20–35; users, defining characteristics 7–8; Western World, relationship **94–95**

social media management: audience engagement 50; authenticity, importance 50; care, display 50; content strategy, creation 50; data-driven social media management 42, 45; goals, defining 48; guidelines 48–50, *49*; influencer marketing, impact 46; online community management 47; outcomes, evaluation 50; paid advertising 46; platform-specific expertise 48; practice *43*, 43–48; professionalization 39–40; sincerity, importance 50; social listening/monitoring techniques, usage 46–47; strategic approach 47–48; target audience, identification 50; visual content, optimization 50

social media platforms 6–7; immediacy/open interactivity 7; information, sharing 68; introduction, chronology **4**; management 37; online community hubs 47; usage 12, 22

social media presence: building 48; early stages 39; handling 40; harnessing (James) 33; image/principles, display 50; impact 11; improvement 48; messaging problems 70; setup 39; sport strengthening 97

social media strategy: creation 39; design 47–48; optimization, data-driven approach (usage) 48; visual content, importance 51

social media users: backlash 73; disparity 86; influencers 8; ladder *8*; newbies, equivalence 8; platform access, mobile devices (usage) 16; problems 97

social monitoring 43, 46–47

social networking: platform, history 5; sites 1–2; websites, development 4

social networks: development 6; social media platform classification 6; types 6; usage 2; usage, practice 22; widening 8

social sex identification 92

social violence 80

socio-cultural issues 1

socio-political advancements 93

space: compression 67; real-world concerns, contrast 76; social media provision 53, 67, 74, 84, 90; sports provision 89

space, predators (anonymity) 76

Spain, Sarah 61; ESPN role 93

spokesperson, athlete role 32

sponsorship 20; activation 27; fostering 39; logo placements, relationship 27; marketing objectives, implementation 21; social media, relationship 26–28; sport media, importance 9

sport: brand, management 20, 23, 25; child sexual abuse, SnapChat (impact) 76–77; clubs, social media (positive space) 75; crisis communication 14; diversity 12–13; emerging issues 9–14; global perspective 62; governing bodies, impact 28–29; inclusion 12–13; Latin

America 56; legal issues 13; legal issues, future 80; male preserve, argument 72–73; media, relationship 54–56; organizations, social media (usage) 9; politics, blogs 59; race, relationship 89; sacred culture perception 76; social media challenges 14–15; social media future, trends **16**; socio-cultural issues 11–12; television, future 57–58; women, participation/denial 93; workplace, feminization 72–73

sport business: management, social media (relationship) 9–10; social media, relationship 20; social media use, elements 20–35

sport industry: social media, future 63, 64; social media management, guidelines 48–50

sporting landscape, protected space 73

sports: amateurism, relationship 89; firms, athletes/sports collaboration 21–22; industry, social media (future) 16–17; loyal listener space 58; male preserve 56; para-sports, visibility (promotion) 12; religion, socio-cultural issue 11; social media, significance 1

stalking, arrests 75

Staples Center (brand association) 24

star athletes, symbolic meaning (transfer) 31

State Farm, Instagram post (Paul) 32

stereotyping (social media challenges) 15

Sterger, Jen (sexual harassment) 59

strategic business medium, service 37

student-athletes: discipline 71; public-facing representatives 72

subreddits, presence 5

Subway: "congratulations" offering, property infringement 29; X usage, coattail ambushing 29–30

suicide prevention, social media space 95

support, social media space 95

symbolic meaning, transfer 31

target audience, identification 50

targeting, enhancement 46

team: loyalty, enhancement/maintenance 25; social media functions 9; social media usage 12

technological drivers 2–3

Tencent, Chinese sport social media (relationship) 57

Thomas, Lia (transgender female) 94

TikTok: introduction 5; usage 2

time compression 67

togetherness, sense (fostering) 12

toxic online environment, fostering 15

trademark infringements 13

traditional media, social media (relationship) 53

Trevor Project, The (website) 95

Trump, Donald (Hill posts) 70–71

Tweddle, Beth (physical threats) 77

tweets, popularity 5

two-way communication 14

UFC TikTok (content community example) 7

UnderArmour, Junior Tour (case study) **63–64**

United States, social media lawsuit (case study) **78–79**

user-generated content, principles 2

user participation, principles 2

user profile (social media platform attribute) 6

US government, Amendment I 68

Valbuena, Mathieu (blackmail) (case study) **78**

value, creation 35

values ambushing 29

video content, popularity (trend) 16

violence: emotional violence 80; inciting 68; sexual violence 80; sexual violence, threats 78, 94; social violence 80; threat 73, 77

visual appeal, leveraging **51**

visual content: importance 51; optimization 50

vlogs presence (YouTube) 5

Wallace, Bubba (tweets) 32

Western World, social media/sexuality (presence/impact) **94–95**

Williams, Serena: physical threats 77; stalking/cyber-bullying 75

women: inclusion, male challenge 94; social media, space (safety)

95–96; sport, participation/denial 93; sports, awareness (raising) 11
workforce, feminization 93
workplace: diversity 73; feminization 72–73
WWE (YouTube channel), content community example 7

"You'll Never Walk Alone" (Liverpool Football Club song) 23
YouTube: content community example 7; influencers 86; introduction 5; launch 4; multi-way conversations, engagement 2; usage 2

For Product Safety Concerns and Information please contact our EU representative GPSR@taylorandfrancis.com
Taylor & Francis Verlag GmbH, Kaufingerstraße 24, 80331 München, Germany

www.ingramcontent.com/pod-product-compliance
Lightning Source LLC
Chambersburg PA
CBHW051755230426
43670CB00012B/2295